# NELSON'S LOVE
# TO LADY HAMILTON

A collection of full text letters
1798 - 1805

## Robert Wickson

First edition published in 2005 by Quest Publications
PO Box 5945 Ferndown BH22 9SW

Copyright 2005 Robert Wickson
ISBN 0-9548822-1-0

# Contents

———○○○———

# *Prologue*

This selection of letters written by Nelson to Lady Hamilton are inevitably one sided. Many of them refer to letters that she sent to him and the reader is naturally intrigued to know what was in them. To put together the letters that they sent to each other would, without doubt, give the reader a much more complete and revealing picture, not only of the love they had for each other, but also a more complete picture of, in particular, the personality of Emma Hamilton.

Unfortunately, this is not possible. The reason being that very few of the letters that Nelson received from Lady Hamilton survived. The clue as to why they did not survive is within these letters – he burned them. Not only did he burn her letters but he urged her to burn his letters also. But Emma could not bring herself to destroy the letters. Nelson's letters to her was the proof of his love and esteem. It was not then surprising that she kept them all.

In Victorian England to read, or possess, the text of letters that confirmed the relationship between Nelson and Lady Hamilton (and especially Horatia, their illegitimate child) was considered to be highly risqué. The sources of the letters in this book were, it seems, a clandestine publication. They were found at the back of a book of Italian verse entitled 'Aminta' by Torquato Tasso, dated 1825. Hence, with the two books bound in one volume, the reader of the Nelson letters, if disturbed, could quickly switch to reading 'Aminta'. Most of the originals of these letters can now be found in the British Library, although there are also many originals that are in private collections.

There are many names mentioned in Nelson's letters that only a wider reading of Nelson's life and history will make clear. But some of the names mentioned are entirely fabricated. As Nelson became suspicious that some of his letters were being opened and read, he arranged with Emma a fictitious couple of 'friends' to write about.

The name chosen was 'Mr Thompson' who was supposed to be member of his crew. Emma was 'Mrs Thompson'. It will be noticed that Nelson was not very good at this deception and gets slightly muddled at times between 'Mr Thompson' and himself.

The deception was carried further, since Horatia was passed off to the world as an 'adopted' daughter, with the name Horatia Nelson Thompson. She was not baptized until 1803, when her date of birth was given as October 27th 1800. This date being about ten days before Nelson and the Hamilton's arrived back in England.

The first of Nelson's letters in this volume is dated 24th October 1798, three months after the Battle of the Nile. Nelson had been staying with the Hamilton's since the 22nd September, but he needed to assess the situation at Malta, which was still in French hands.

It is fairly formal and business like. He addresses her as 'My Dear Madam'. They were not, at that time, lovers. But it will be noticed that there is a marked difference between this letter and those that follow. He changes to 'My Dear Lady Hamilton' by May 1799; (it is reputed that they first made love in February 1799) then 'My Dearest Friend' and, in 1803, 'My Dearest Emma' until his final letter 'My Dearest Beloved Emma and Dear Friend of my Bosom' written on October 19th 1805, which he left unfinished just before the Battle of Trafalgar. But it will be noted that his most intimate letters were not headed with any name and he did not sign them. This device might have put any other reader off the scent if he had bothered to also disguise his handwriting. But strangely, considering the other deceptions that they arranged between them, he made no effort to change the way he wrote.

In his correspondence, Nelson sometimes refers to himself in the third person, as though the public Nelson, the national hero, was a separate being. Essentially though, this book is confined to the private Nelson. As such it is an important part of the history of Nelson's life from the start of his relationship with Lady Hamilton until his death seven years later. The letters confirm the deep and passionate love he had for the wife of his best friend, Sir William Hamilton. They also reveal Nelson as the ordinary man, a very human being.

Although it is not possible to present the letters in Nelson's own handwriting, which, since the loss of his right arm, was sometimes difficult to read, they are presented in a 'handwritten' style that is similar to that of the eighteenth century. In this way it is hoped to recall some of the spontaneity and privacy that handwritten letters convey to the reader.

It might also be mentioned that although the text of Nelson's letters have been faithfully adherred to, some leniency has has been tacken with paragraphs and spacing.Nelson's actual letters were much more compact and usually written from edge to edge, without margins. He did not waste much paper with spaces.

To Anna & William
with best regards

Robert Wichson.
Oct. 21. 2005.

# A short profile of Emma, Lady Hamilton

**The events leading up to her introduction to Nelson in 1793, together with a short account of their association between 1798 and 1805.**

It was on the 26th April 1765 that Mary Lyon presented her husband Henry with a baby daughter. She was named Amy. They lived in the Wirral, Cheshire.

Historians have given Henry Lyon various occupations, ranging from collier, blacksmith, tanner and the like but, whatever it was, there is no doubt that it was hard work that did not pay well. Henry Lyon died when Amy was about five years old. Amy then went to live with her grandmother, Mrs Kidd, who lived across the border at Harwarden, in North Wales. As soon as Amy was old enough to be taken on, she was put into domestic service. She was then probably eight or nine years old.

As she approached her thirteenth birthday it was clear that she was developing into an attractive young woman. At about this time she came to London, accompanied by her mother, and was again put 'into service'. But as the months past by and Amy continued to develop, it seems that her mother (or Amy herself) came up with the idea of either finding a rich husband, or otherwise to exploit her natural beauty in some way.

Within a year, exploitation seems to have been the main purpose, since Amy is then known to have been employed as a 'Goddess of Health' by a Dr Graham, who lectured at the Adelphi on the 'medical' properties of such things as drinking spa water, taking mud baths and taking exercise.

Amy posed nude on a pedestal in various classical 'attitudes' during the lectures as the living proof of all he said. The classical 'attitudes' she developed and later they came in useful as her own particular 'party piece' – but with clothes on.

Whether or not well-to-do Captain John Willet Payne (a friend of the Prince of Wales, another noted womaniser) was among the audience to observe and admire the new luscious 'Goddess of Health' is not known, but it is he who is reputed to have first 'bedded' Amy. She was then almost fifteen years old.

Shortly after, she is then known to have become the mistress of Sir Harry Featherstonhaugh and, under the guise of going back 'into service', was taken by him to live at his country house, Up Park, in Sussex. The 'service' she provided for Sir Harry was, then, mainly in the bedchamber.

Sir Harry treated her well, was not mean with spending money and Amy enjoyed the life whilst it lasted. But unfortunately it did not last, since Amy became pregnant, resulting in Sir Harry swiftly tipping her out.

Amy went back to her grandmother in Harwarden, where she gave birth to a daughter who was named Emma – thereafter referred to as 'little Emma'.

Leaving little Emma with her grandmother, Amy returned to London and changed her name to Emly Hart. She then turned to the only person she had previously met (in what circumstances is not known) that might help her. His name was Charles Greville MP, who was the youngest son of the Earl of Warwick and whose mother was the sister of Sir William Hamilton, the British Envoy in Naples

It was April, and on the 26th she had her seventeenth birthday. The new Emly Hart was now the live in mistress of Charles Greville, aged thirty-three. In addition, her mother was taken on as his housekeeper. Before long Emly was being called 'Emma' and this was the name that remained with her.

In fact, it was to turn out that, from this point on, for the rest of her life, Emma was not only to be the provider of a roof for her own head, but also provider of a roof and a comfortable living for her widowed mother. Wherever Emma went, mother went too. Her mother also changed her name to Mrs Cadogan.

Charles Greville was not rich; he had an allowance of £500 a year from his father and, possibly, other small sources of income, such as managing his uncle's estate in Wales. But they lived together in harmony for four years, during which time Greville taught Emma not only to read and write, but paid for her to have piano and singing lessons.

Although their social life was restricted - Greville, being a 'gentleman' and an aristocrat, could not be seen openly in public with his mistress, it would have been social suicide – but he did introduce her to certain of his trusted 'avant-garde' friends.

One such friend was the portrait painter George Romney, who was immediately smitten by Emma's beauty. He declared that she was one of the most beautiful women he had ever met.

He painted her so many times that it was often said that every painting of a female he did thereafter bore some resemblance to his favourite model.

But after four years the burden of keeping up his own appearances as well as providing for a mistress and her mother was straining his limited income. After all, it was not just food and shelter he had to provide, it was clothing and all the other living expenses for the three of them, or rather, four, since Greville was also paying £20 per year for the upkeep of 'little Emma'.

It was also fashionable for his social standing at the time to indulge in some form of gambling, however moderate this might be. Later, in Naples, Emma was also to show herself to be a keen gambler at cards. Whether Greville or Sir William taught her the gambling habit is not known, but what is known is that whoever it was, she played with their money (and, later, Nelson's too) and did not often win.

And so Greville gradually got into debt, and the only way he could see out of his predicament was to marry 'into money'. At some time it also dawned upon him that to get out of his predicament of debt, he had to face the predicament of what to do about Emma. He could not go courting for a rich spouse whilst at the same time supporting a live in mistress and her mother. Somehow, he had to ditch Emma and her mother, before he could assume the role of a virtuous and eligible bachelor once again. Also, it would not do if he tipped Emma out and she became the mistress of one of his friends or acquaintances (he probably mused that the painter George Romney was a definite possibility!)

No, he had to get Emma not only out of his house but also out of London. Better still, out of England altogether. What better then, than shipping her off to his uncle in Naples! At first, although a widower for some years, and one who had admired his nephew's mistress when on leave, Sir William Hamilton was very reluctant to take on a twenty year old nymph, who would seem more like his daughter - or even granddaughter.

But Charles Greville was very persuasive and, eventually, his uncle gave in.

Greville could not bring himself to tell Emma of his true intentions. He told her that he was planning to visit his uncle William in Italy and she was to go with him. She must have been thrilled. But in the last days before departure, Greville had 'urgent business' to attend to that prevented him from sailing with her. She was not to be disappointed by having to wait for him; he would join her as soon as he could. And she would not be alone, mother was going too.

Once again, Emma was to enter a new chapter in her life on her birthday. She and her mother reached Naples on April 26th 1786; she was twenty-one. She was enthralled by all she saw. But she missed her lover and wrote to him imploring him to hurry to her. And she wrote many times. Gradually, it dawned upon her that he was not coming. She was devastated to have lost her first true love but, with Sir Williams's kindness and indulgence to fall back on, she started to enjoy being admired by Neapolitan society. Not that she could be accepted at Court, even though the Queen was civil to her, it was at a distance.

Although Emma had raged at Charles Greville that she would never share the same bed with Sir William, after three years in his company, together with the growing awareness of his close relationship with the King and Queen of Naples, and the pleasant lifestyle she was enjoying, at some point she changed her mind and became his mistress.

She then started to spread the rumour that they were, secretly, married anyway. The easy going Sir William was not upset, even when he heard that the rumour had reached England. He was not against marrying Emma, but more concerned that, having married her and made her officially and legally 'Lady Hamilton', she would still not be accepted by the Court of Naples. This problem was resolved when the Queen indicated that, as Lady Hamilton, Emma would certainly be accepted in Court Circles.

It was two years later, early in September 1791, back in England on leave, Sir William Hamilton finally married Emma at Marylebone Church. Charles Greville was in attendance to wish his uncle and his new aunt well. She was twenty-six, Sir William was sixty-one. In November 1791 the Hamilton's returned to Italy through France.

In Paris, as the new Lady Hamilton, Emma was presented to the French Queen, Marie Antoinette, who gave her a letter to take to her sister, Queen Maria Carolina, in Naples.(They were the daughters of Queen Marie Theresa of the Austrian Hapsberg's) Upon their return to Naples, Emma devoted herself to playing the part of the wife of the British Envoy. She not only became popular at Court, she became a close friend of Queen Maria Carolina. Any travellers from Britain, who desired an audience with the Queen, had to first approach the wife of the British Envoy, Emma, Lady Hamilton. Speaking, by that time, fluent Italian, Emma had also become a 'confidante' of the Queen.

In October 1793, Marie Antoinette went to the guillotine. A French army was on the march across Europe and so it was not surprising that the King and Queen of Naples began to fear an attack by France. Although the Austrian army gave them some protection from land attack, Naples was also vulnerable from attack by sea.

It was in 1793 that Nelson first met the Hamilton's. In September he brought despatches from England to assure King Ferdinand and the Queen of the protection of the British navy.  Sir William and Lady Hamilton invited him to stay with them during his visit. He introduced his stepson Josiah Nisbet to them, who was then a midshipman on his ship, then sailed away after five days. His next visit was to be five years later. Nelson was to remark in a letter to his wife that Sir William was '…a man after my own heart' and Lady Hamilton as '…. kind and amiable and very good to Josiah.'

Just as Lady Hamilton was following and enjoying her new role as the wife of the British Envoy, Nelson was continuing his own stated quest for 'glory'. Between 1793 and 1797 Nelson was engaged in the harassing and blockading of French ports. In July 1794 he lost the sight of his right eye in a land action on Corsica. During this time his ship was provisioned at Leghorn and (as Emma was later to find out), he had a mistress there. Her name was Adelaide Correglia, an opera singer with a 'reputation'.

 By October 1796, the French advances in Europe towards Italy finally decided Spain to join with France against the British. With a combined French and Spanish fleet against them, together with fewer bases from which to operate, orders were sent to the British fleet to withdraw from the Mediterranean.

Upon leaving the Mediterranean, the British fleet, cruising off the coast of Portugal near Cape St Vincent, came upon the Spanish fleet and, even though outnumbered, decided to attack. Nelson distinguished himself by disobeying orders but ending up being the hero of the battle. Breaking out of line he was in action against five Spanish warships for an hour. His ship was a wreck, but he rammed into the back of the 80 gun *San Nicolas*, boarded her through the rear windows and took the ship. As the *San Nicolas* had become tangled up with another first rate, the 112 gun *San Josef,* Nelson called for more boarders and jumped across with them. After a short skirmish the Spanish captain surrendered to Nelson and presented his sword.

Nelson's Commander-in-Chief, Sir John Jervis, was created Earl St Vincent and Nelson was made a Knight of the Bath and promoted to rear admiral. He was the talk of the nation and the nations hero. His wife, Fanny, was not so impressed and begged him not to go boarding again and to '*...leave it to the Captains'* in the future.

Hearing news of a Spanish treasure ship heading for Tenerife, Jervis thought he would reward Nelson by sending him to capture the treasure. The action took place on 25th July 1797 and ended in disaster. Josiah, his stepson, (now a lieutenant) was to save Nelson's life when his arm was shot off during the attack on Santa Cruz. It was Nelson's most humiliating defeat.

With the loss of his arm, Nelson thought that his career in the navy was over.

He wrote to Admiral Sir John Jervis the new Earl St. Vincent, *'I am become a burthen to my friends, and useless to my country....A left-handed Admiral will never again be considered as useful, therefore the sooner I get to a very humble cottage the better....'* He added a request to promote his stepson to Captain, which was granted by making him Captain of the hospital ship that brought him back to England. (Josiah was to fail miserably as a Captain and eventually left the navy)

Nelson arrived back in England on 1st September 1797. Crowds gathered to cheer him wherever he went. His wife, Fanny, nursed him back to good health and they bought a house called Roundwood, near Ipswich, for £2000.

In January 1798 he advised the Admiralty that he was fit for service once again. By the end of March he was hoisting his flag on the '*Vanguard'* at Portsmouth and four weeks later he joined up with Earl St. Vincent and the British fleet blockading Cadiz. With just two 74-gun ships of the line and three frigates Nelson was sent back into the Mediterranean to reconnoitre.

Shortly after, St Vincent sent ten more 74's after him, with the orders to seek out and destroy the French fleet by whatever methods he considered necessary.

For three months, Nelson chased around the Mediterranean trying to find Napoleon Bonaparte's invasion fleet. In the meantime, the King and Queen of Naples, frightened of invasion, had declared themselves neutral. In practical terms this meant that the British fleet was barred from being provisioned at Naples.

Nelson sent Captain Thomas Troubridge ashore to speak to Sir William Hamilton. Sir William took Captain Troubridge to see Sir John Acton, (who acted as King Ferdinand's 'Prime Minister') who wrote a directive to the governors of Sicily to supply the British fleet.

Lady Hamilton was later to claim that it was her influence with the Queen that obtained the directive to the governors of Sicily to supply the British fleet. She always hoped this would lead to a pension from the British government, but it never transpired. If she did intervene, the evidence is missing, even though, later, Nelson was to give some support to her claim.

The British knew that Bonaparte had put to sea but did not know his destination. It was then found that he had captured Malta and then sailed on. Not until the French fleet was discovered anchored in Aboukir Bay, Alexandria, late in the afternoon of August 1st 1798 was it realised that Bonaparte had landed his army in Egypt.

Having spent so long searching, Nelson, in spite of the lateness of the day, decided to attack. He had already explained his proposed tactics to his captains - his 'band of brothers.' The battle went on into the night and finally ended with the French flagship blowing up - the battle was won

The destruction of the French fleet had isolated Bonaparte's army in Egypt. For the time being, Naples and the rest of Europe could breath again.

His ship, badly damaged, limped back to Naples where, on the 22nd September, he was greeted by the King and the Hamilton's.

Emma, clambering on board the ship first, flung herself onto Nelson's remaining arm and declared 'O God, is it possible!'

He must have noticed that, in the space of the five years since his last visit she had become quite an armful, since she had put on some weight. But she was still a voluptuous woman and the contact was probably (and perhaps calculated to be) not unwelcome to a man so long at sea.

In spite of still being exhausted and still suffering from a head wound, celebrations, dinners and entertainments had been laid on for the conquering hero, and he and all his officers were swept up in it. And Emma nursed and fussed over Nelson like a mother.

On September 30th 1798 Nelson wrote to Lord St Vincent:

' I trust, my Lord, in a week we shall be at sea. I am very unwell, and the miserable conduct of this Court is not likely to cool my irritable temper. It is a country of fiddlers and poets, whores and scoundrels'.

But Nelson did not go. The letters in this volume start on October 24th 1798, almost three months after the Battle of the Nile. Nelson is writing about the situation in Malta. He left ships there to blockade the harbour under Captain Ball and sailed back to Naples, which was to be his base for the next twenty-one months. In November, news arrived that Nelson had been created Baron Nelson of the Nile

His new friends, Sir William and Lady Hamilton, sucked him into an existence that he had never known before. The hero worship lavished upon Nelson by Lady Hamilton was not only condoned but also shared and encouraged by Sir William. No small favour or pleasure was to be denied the hero of the day. In a letter to his nephew Sir William was to remark that; 'Lord Nelson and I, with Emma, are the 'tria juncta in uno'…..I glory in the hospitality I have in my power to show Lord Nelson and almost all the heroes of the Nile'.

(But, two months later, he was writing to complain about the expense of it all.)

At Naples, Nelson did not remain idle. He urged the Court of Naples to raise an army and march on Rome. The Court appointed General Mack and, with King Ferdinand at the head, marched and entered Rome on the 26th November. The victory was very short-lived. The expected help of the Austrian army from the north was refused. The French counter-attacked within weeks and King Ferdinand and the remains of his army scuttled back to Naples.

In spite of vowing to the people of Naples that they would stay, the King and Queen secretly made plans with Nelson to take them to their second kingdom, Sicily. Emma was to play a significant role in the plans to leave Naples. In those days, if it could be avoided, a Royal Family did not abscond without taking its treasure chest and a lot of baggage.

Emma saw to it that all the baggage was safely labelled (as 'provisions' for Nelson) and taken from the Royal Palace in covered wagons to the Hamilton's Palazzo Sessa, from where Emma had discovered a secret tunnel to the shore. Over several days, Nelson's men carried the baggage out to the waiting ships. On the evening of the 21st December, they all attended a reception given by the Turkish Envoy, but gradually slipped away to make for the quay and the waiting boats.

It was to be a terrifying journey in violent storms. One of Queen Carolina's children (she had thirteen), the six-year-old Prince Carlo took ill and died in Emma's arms on Christmas day; they reached Palermo on Boxing Day. Four weeks later the French entered Naples.

It was probably at Palermo that Nelson and Lady Hamilton first made love. The likely date was 11th February 1799; a date that Nelson was later to remark brought back fond memories, with no regrets. But, whenever they made love, it was probably not all that often. They had to be careful to maintain the appearance of being just close friends, but not 'stepping over the line'. And so the formalities of good appearance, of '*bienseance*' were strictly observed. If Sir William was suspicious, he threw a blind eye to it.

For his services, King Ferdinand created Nelson Duke of Bronte, with an estate of approximately 30,000 acres, of mostly barren land, at the foot of Mount Etna, Sicily. His residence at Bronte was previously a monastery and the rental income, he was told, was £3000 per annum. There is no evidence that he ever went to see his estate on Sicily, or that he ever received any rent.

Although Nelson bequeathed to Emma £500 a year from his Bronte estate, she never received it.

By this time Nelson and the Hamilton's were inseparable. Also, Nelson's 'friendship' with Emma Hamilton was becoming widely talked about. His good friend Captain Troubridge wrote to Nelson and bluntly told him that the late night card games and gaming that went on after Sir William had long gone to bed was damaging to both his reputation, as well as that of Lady Hamilton. After that the card games stopped, but not the gossip.

In July 1800 Nelson was finally granted leave. Sir William was now retired and his replacement had arrived. They decided to travel together to England overland through Europe. They were feted, dined and wined wherever they stopped. On the way they met Lord and Lady Minto, who later remarked that Nelson was led around by Emma '..like a keeper with a bear'. They reached England on 6th November and landed at Great Yarmouth.

If Nelson had any hopes of an 'understanding' between his wife Fanny and Emma Hamilton, they were quickly dashed. Although Emma had put on weight and tried to disguise it, she could not disguise the fact from any other woman that she was seven months pregnant. Nelson split with his wife. He wrote to the Admiralty asking for an immediate return to duty. As there was talk of Bonaparte planning an invasion of England, the Admiralty appointed him second-in-command of the Channel Fleet, with the rank of Vice-Admiral. His Commander-in-Chief was Lord St Vincent.

By the 28th January 1801 he had joined his new ship the *San Josef* at Plymouth. The birth of their daughter, Horatia, is calculated to have been on the 30th January. (a letter on the 3rd February refers to 'a dear little girl').

After the split with his wife, Nelsons letters during 1801 become more intimate. On the 1st March, he wrote one of his most passionate letters, starting with *'Now, my dear wife, for such you are in my eyes and in the face of heaven…..'* This letter, although delivered by a trusted messenger by hand, was, like many others, not headed and not signed. Later in 1801 he urges Emma to seek out a suitable house near to London where they can all live together. In September, relying upon Emma's advice, he buys Merton Place, in Surrey, about seven miles from the Admiralty. The house needed many alterations and improvements, but he was pleased enough when, on the 26th October he was granted leave and saw Merton for the first time. He had borrowed money from his friend and agent, Alexander Davison in order to buy Merton, but the 'tria juncta in uno' were now living together under one roof. For the time being there was peace with France. Nelson and the Hamilton's lived together for the next eighteen months. They went on a trip to Wales to see Sir Williams estate there. Nelson was cheered and feted at each town that he went through. In Monmouth, they erected a monument.

Back at Merton they had a continuous stream of Nelson's family and friends to stay or dine with them. So much so that Sir William eventually began to complain and tensions began to mount. Unable to communicate his feelings directly to Emma, he wrote to her. The friction between them must stop, he said, because he did not wish it to spread to make Nelson unhappy. They must 'live and let live'. All he wanted was to go fishing, visit his club and take it easy. He was also, by now, short of money.

Sir William died on the 6th April 1803. On the 16th May, Nelson was called back to active service upon the renewal of hostilities with France.

He was made Commander-in-Chief of the Mediterranean fleet. He joined the fleet at Toulon in July and hoisted his flag on the *Victory*. Just out of sight of land, he waited for the French fleet to put to sea. It was to be a long wait.

To keep a fleet at sea, always ready for action, adequately provisioned and with a healthy crew was a continuous challenge. There were few friendly ports to call at. For long months he prowled around the Mediterranean. His reputation was such that no enemy Admiral wished to confront him. It was not until April 1805 that he had news that the French fleet had slipped out of the Mediterranean. But where had it gone? Not to join the Spanish fleet at Cadiz, not into the English Channel and, he guessed, not to Ireland. The only other possible route was the West Indies. Without hesitation, Nelson set out. He had guessed correctly, but he did not manage to catch up with them. He chased them back to Cadiz, and Nelson stepped ashore at Gibraltar, after two years at sea. On the 18th August 1805, Nelson and the *Victory* arrived back at Portsmouth, and he lost no time in getting back to Merton, where Emma was waiting for him. Two weeks later he rejoined his ship and met up with his fleet once again off Cadiz on 28th September.

He had urged the Admiralty and the newspapers in England and Gibraltar not to mention that he had rejoined the fleet. The combined French and Spanish fleets finally met with the British fleet on the 21st October 1805 off Cape Trafalgar. Nelson was mortally wounded. He lived long enough to learn that the battle was won, 'Thank God, I have done my duty', he whispered.

As he lay dying, he had only one wish – that his country would look after Lady Hamilton. History reveals that, in the corridors of power, for the sake of *bienseance*, it was a wish too far.

My Dear Madam,

After a long passage, we are arrived; and it is as I suspected — the ministers at Naples know nothing of the situation of the island. Not a house or bastion of the town is in possession of the islanders; and the Marquis de Niza tells me, they want arms, victuals and support. He does not know, that any Neapolitan officers are in the island; perhaps, although I have their names, none are arrived; and it is very certain, by the Marquis's account, that no supplies have been sent by the Governors of Syracuse or Messina.

However, I shall and will know everything as soon as the Marquis is gone, which will be tomorrow morning. He says, he is very anxious to serve under my command; and by changing his ship, it appears as if he was so, however, I understand the trim of our English ships better.

Ball will have the management of the blockade after my departure; as it seems, the Court of Naples think my presence may be necessary, and useful, in the beginning of November.

I hope it will prove so; but, I feel, my duty lays at present in the East; for, until I know the shipping in Egypt are destroyed, I shall never consider the French army as completely sure of never returning to Europe.

However, all my views are to serve and save the Two Sicilies; and to do that which their Majesties may wish me, even against my own opinion, when I come to Naples, and that country is at war. I shall wish to have a meeting with General Acton on this subject.

You will, I am sure, do me justice with the Queen; for I declare to God, my whole study is, how best to meet her approbation.

God bless you and Sir William! and ever believe me, with the most affectionate regard, your obliged and faithful friend,

Horatio Nelson

I may possibly, but this is not certain, send in the enclosed letter.

Shew it to Sir William, This must depend on what I hear and see; for I believe scarcely anything I hear.

Once more, God bless you!

12

My Dear Lady Hamilton,

Accept my sincere thanks for your kind letter. Nobody writes so well; therefore, pray, say not you write ill; for, if you do, I will say — what your goodness sometimes told me — "You l — e!" I can read, and perfectly understand, every word you write.

We drank your and Sir William's health. Troubridge, Louis, Hallowell, and the new Portuguese captain, dined here.

I shall soon be at Palermo; for this business must very soon be settled. No one, believe me, is more sensible of your regard, than your obliged and grateful

Nelson.

I am pleased with little Mary; kiss her for me. I thank all the house for their regard. God bless you all!

I shall send on shore, if fine, to-morrow; for the feluccas are going to leave us, and I am sea sick. I have got the piece of wood for the tea-chest; it shall soon be sent.

Pray, present my humble duty and gratitude to the Queen, for all her marks of regard; and assure her, it is not thrown away on an ungrateful soil.

"Vanguard" May 19, 1799
Eight o'clock. Calm

My Dear Lady Hamilton

Lieutenant Swiney coming on board, enables me to send some blank passports for vessels going to Procida with corn, etc., and also one for the courier boat. To tell you, how dreary and uncomfortable the Vanguard appears, is only telling you, what it is to go from the pleasantest society to a solitary cell; or, from the dearest friends, to no friends. I am now perfectly the Great Man — not a creature near me.

From my heart I wish myself the little man again!

You, and good Sir William, have spoiled me for any place but with you. I love Mrs Cadogan.

You cannot conceive what I feel, when I call you all to my remembrance. Even to Mira, do not forget your faithful and affectionate

Nelson

My Dear Lady Hamilton,

Many thanks to you and Sir William for your kind notes. You will believe I did not sleep much, with all my letters to read, etc., etc.

My letters from Lord St Vincent are May 6th. He says — "We saw the Brest squadron pass us yesterday, under an easy sail. I am making every effort to get information to Lord Keith; Who I have ordered here, to complete their water and provisions. I conjecture, the French squadron is bound for Malta and Alexandria; and the Spanish fleet for the attack on Minorca".

I must leave you to judge, whether the Earl will come to us. I think he will; but 'entre nous', Mr Duckworth means to leave me to my fate.

I send you (under all circumstances) his letter. Never mind; if I can get my eleven sail together, they shall not hurt me.

God bless you, Sir William, and all our joint friends in your house; Noble, Gibbs, etc., and believe me ever, for ever, your affectionate friend,

Nelson

My Dear Lady Hamilton

Having a Commander-in-Chief, I cannot come on shore until I have made my manners to him. Times are changed; but, if he does not come on shore directly, I will not wait.

In the meantime I send Allen to enquire how you are. Send me word, for I am anxious to hear of you. It has been no fault of mine that I have been so long absent. I cannot command; and, now, only obey.

Mr Tyson, and the Consul, have not been able to find the betrothed wife of the Priore; although they were three days in their inquiries, and desired the Neapolitan Consul to send to Pisa.

I also desired the Russian Admiral, as he was going to Pisa, to inquire if the Countess Pouschkin had any letters to send to Palermo; but as I received none, I take it for granted she had none to send.

May God bless you, my dear Lady: and be assured, I ever am, and shall be, your obliged and affectionate

Bronte Nelson

February 13th, 1800

I do not send you any news or opinions, as this letter goes by post and may be opened, and as I wrote to you and Sir William yesterday, nothing particular has occurred. We are now off Messina with a fresh breeze and fair. Mr Roche has had the goodness to come on board.

To say how I miss your house and company would be saying little, but in truth you and Sir William have so spoiled me that I am not happy anywhere else but with you, nor have I an idea that I ever can be. All my newspapers are purloined at Gibraltar, and I suspect a gentleman there has sent them to Lord Keith, for they are all stars. I see in Lord Grenville's note to Paris he concludes with saying that the best mode he can recommend for France to have a solid peace is to replace its ancient princes on the thrown. May the Heavens bless you and make you ever be satisfied that I am, &c.,

You will make my kindest regards to Sir William and to all the house, also duty to the Queen.

18th February 1800

I feel anxious to get up with these ships & shall be unhappy not to take them myself, for first my greatest happiness is to serve my King and Country, and I am envious only of glory: for if it be a sin to covet glory I am the most offending sole alive. But here I am in a heavy sea & thick fog — Oh God! the wind subsided — but I trust to Providence I shall have them.

18th, in the evening, I have got her — 'Le Genereux' — thank God!

12 out of 13, only the ' Guillaume Telle' remaining: I am after the others. I have not suffered the French Admiral to contaminate the 'Foudroyant' by setting foot in her.

My Dear Lady Hamilton,

Had you seen the Peer receive me, I know not what you would have done; but, I can guess. But never mind!

I told him, that I had made a vow, if I took the 'Genereux' by myself, it was my intention to strike my flag. To which he made no answer.

If I am well enough, I intend to write a letter to Prince Leopold, and to send him the French Admiral's flag; which I hope you will approve of, as it was taken on the coast of his father's kingdom, and by as faithful a subject as any in his dominions.

I have had no communications with the shore: therefore, have seen neither Ball, Troubridge, or Graham: nor with the Lion; when I have, I shall not forget all your messages, and little Jack.

I only want to know your wishes, that I may, at least, appear grateful, by attending them.

My head aches dreadfully, and I have none here to give me a moment's comfort.

I send the packet to General Acton; as I think it may go quicker, and he will be flattered by presenting the flag and letter to the Prince.

Malta, I think, will fall soon, if these other corvettes do not get in.

Pray, make my best regards acceptable to Mrs Cadogan, Miss Knight, little Mary Re Giovanni, Gibbs, etc., etc., and ever believe me your truly faithful and affectionate

Bronte Nelson

My Dear Lady Hamilton

What a difference — but it was to be — from your house to a boat!

Fresh breeze of wind, the ship four or five leagues from the mole; getting on board into a truly hog-style of a cabin, leaking like a sieve, consequently floating with water. What a change!

Not a felucca near us. I saw them come out this morning, but they think there is too much wind and swell.

Pray, do not keep the cutter; as I have not a thing, if anything important should arrive, to send you.

Only think of Tyson's being left!

May God bless you, my dear lady; and believe me, ever, your truly affectionate friend,

Nelson

Lady Hamilton — Put the candlestick on _my_ writing-table

If you'll believe me, nothing can give me so much pleasure as your truly kind and friendly letters, and where friendship is of so strong a cast as ours, it is no easy matter to shake it — mine is as fixed as Mount Etna, and as warm in the inside as that mountain.

The 'Audacious', Gould, will be paid off tomorrow, and he bears the talking of Miss Knight with good humour. He has inquired where she lives. He is not grown much wiser since we left him, or he never would have wished to leave such a ship and ship's company. I am quite vexed not to have orders for completing the San Josef's complement of men, or to proceed to sea, therefore I shall certainly not be at Torbay on Wednesday. I shall write to Troubridge this day to send me your letter, which I look for as constantly and with more anxiety than my dinner.

(Let her go to Brighton or where she pleases, I care not: she is a great fool, and, thank God! you are not the least bit like her.

I delivered poor Mrs Thompson's note; her friend is truly thankful for her kindness and your goodness. Who does not admire your benevolent heart. Poor man! He is very anxious, and begs you will, if she is not able, write a line just to comfort him. He appears to me to feel very much her situation; he is so agitated, and will be so for 2 or 3 days, that he says he cannot write, and that I must send his kind love and affectionate regards.)

What dreadful weather we have got: a deep snow. I wish I was just setting off for Bronte. I should then be happy. As I cannot now sail before Thursday, you may direct your letter on Tuesday to me at Plymouth, and if ever so ready will not sail till the post is arrived.

On Wednesday direct to Brixham as I mentioned before, and believe me as ever, your obliged attached, & most affectionate friend, &c,

My brother is as vexed as I am, and fears he shall lose his trip to Torbay. I should have lived on board before, but, as the ship will be paid tomorrow, I hope to get on board on Tuesday. I hate Plymouth.

I shall write every day.

When I consider that this day nine months was your birthday, and that although we had a gale of wind, yet I was happy, and sung Come Cheer up Fair Emma, &c. Even the thoughts compared with this day make me melancholy, my heart is somehow sunk within me. I long to hear you are well (keep up your spirits, all will end well), the dearest of friends must part, and we only part, I trust, to meet again. (I own I wonder that Sir Wm. should have a wish for the Prince of Wales to come under your roof; no good can come of it, but every harm. You are too beautiful not to have any enemies, and even one visit will stamp you as his chere amie, and we know he is dotingly fond of such women as yourself, and is without one spark of honour in these respects, and would leave you to bewail your folly. But, my dear friend, I know you too well not to be convinced you cannot be seduced by any prince in Europe. You are, in my opinion the pattern of perfection.)

I have no orders, and can have none before Wednesday, therefore sooner than Thursday or Friday the ship cannot move. I have told my brother of your intention to give him a paste. (He would have had a hard matter to get one of mine.) He proposes, if no orders arrive very soon, to leave me, when I shall instantly return on board. I feel no loss at not going to these balls and assemblies. My thoughts are very differently engaged. I know nothing of my destination more than I did in London, but the papers and reports of my being put in a bad ship which, although I can hardly credit, fills me with sorrow, which, joined to my private feelings, makes me this day ready to burst every moment into tears. I will try and write to the Duke tomorrow; this day I could not if millions lay in my way. Mrs Thompson's friend is this moment come into the room. He desires me to thank you for your goodness to his friend.

He appears almost as miserable as myself. He says you have always been kind to his dear Mrs Thompson, and he hopes you will continue your goodness to her on this trying occasion. I have assured him of your innate worth and affectionate disposition, and believe, as ever and ever, your, &c.

My best respects to Sir William, Mrs Denis, &c., &c.

What a fool I was, my dear Lady Hamilton,

- to direct that your cheering letters should be directed for Brixham! I feel, this day, truly miserable, in not having them; and, I fear, they will not come till tomorrow's post.

What a blockhead, to believe any person is so active as myself! I have this day got my orders to put myself under Lord St Vincent's command; but, as no order is arrived to man the ship, it must be Friday night, or Saturday morning, before she can sail for Torbay. Direct my letters, now, to Brixham.

My eye is very bad. I have had the physician of the fleet to examine it. He has directed me not to write, (and yet I am forced, this day, to write to Lord Spencer, St Vincent, Davidson about my lawsuit, Troubridge, Mr Locker, etc., but you are the only female I write to;) not to eat anything but the most simple food; to have green shades for my eyes — (will you, my dear friend, make me one or two? Nobody else shall;) — and to bath them in cold water every hour.

I fear, it is the writing has brought on this complaint. My eye is like blood; and the film so extended, that I only see from the corner farthest from my nose.

What a fuss about my complaints! But, being so far from my sincere friends, I have leisure to brood over them.

I have this moment seen Mrs Thompson's friend. Poor fellow! He seems very uneasy and melancholy. He begs you to be kind to her; and I have assured him of your readiness to relieve the dear good woman: and believe me for ever, my dear Lady, your faithful, attached, and affectionate

*Nelson & Bronte*

I will try and write the Duke a line. My brother intended to have gone off to-morrow afternoon; but this half order may stop him.

Your good and dear friend, does not think it proper at present to write with his own hand (but he hopes the time may not be far distant when he may be united for ever to the object of his wishes, his only love. He swears before heaven that he will marry you as soon as it is possible, which he fervently prays may be soon.) He charges me to say how dear you are to him, and that you must, every opportunity, kiss and bless for him his dear little girl, which he wishes to be called Emma, out of gratitude to our dear, good Lady Hamilton; but in either its from Lord N. he says, or Lady H., he leaves to your judgment and choice. I have given Lord N. a hundred pounds this morning, for which he will give Lady Hamilton an order on his agents; and I beg that you will distribute it amongst those who have been useful to you on the late occasion; and your friend, my dear Mrs Thompson, may be sure of my care of him and his interest, which I consider as dearly as my own, and do you believe me ever, &c.,

Lady Hamilton must desire at the back for it to be paid to the person who carries it.

February 5th, 1801

Your dear and excellent friend has desired me to say that it is not usual to christen children till they are a month or six weeks old; and as Lord Nelson will probably be in town, as well as myself, before we go to the Baltic, he proposes then, if you approve, to christen the child, and that myself and Lady Hamilton should be two of the sponsors. It can be christened at St. George's, Hanover Square; and, I believe, the parents being at the time out of the kingdom, if it is necessary, it can be stated born at Portsmouth or at sea. Its name will be Horatia, daughter of Johem and Morata Etnorb. If you read the surname backwards, and take the letters of the other names, it will make, very extraordinary, the names of your real and affectionate friends, Lady Hamilton and myself; but, my dear friend consult with Lady Hamilton. Your friend consults me, and I would not lead him wrong for the world; he has not been very well: I believe he has fretted, but his spirit is too high to own it. But, my dear Madam, both him, you, and your little one, must always believe me your affectionate, &c.

The child, if you like it, can be named by any clergyman without its going to church.

San Josef,
February 8th, 1801

My Dear Lady,

Mr Davidson demands the privilege of carrying back an answer to your kind letter; and I am sure, he will be very punctual in the delivery.

I am not in very good spirits; and, except that our country demands all our services and abilities, to bring about an honourable peace, nothing should prevent me being the bearer of my own letter. But, my dear friend, I know you are so true and loyal an Englishwomen, that you would hate those who would not stand forth in defence of our King, laws, religion and all that is dear to us.

It is you sex that makes us go forth; and seem to tell us — "None but the brave deserve the fair!" and if we all fail, we still live in the hearts of those females.

You are dear to us. It is your sex that rewards us; It is your sex who cherish our memories; and you, my dear, honoured friend, are, believe me, the _first_, the best, of your sex.

I have been the world around, and in every corner of it and never yet saw your equal, or even one which could be put in comparison with you. You know how to reward virtue, honour, and courage; and never to ask if it is placed in a Prince, Duke, Lord, or peasant: and I hope, one day, to see you, in peace, before I set out for Bronte, which I am resolved to do.

Darby's is one of the ships sent out after the French squadron; I shall, therefore, give the print to Hardy. I think, they may come by the mail-coach, as a parcel; wrapped up round a stick; any print shop will give you one: and direct it as my letters. The coach stops, for parcels, at the White Bear, I believe Piccadilly. Pray have you got any picture from Mrs Heads? I hope Mr Brydon has executed the frames to your satisfaction; the will, he is directed to send to me.

Only tell me, how I can be useful to you and Sir William; and believe nothing could give me more pleasure: being with the greatest truth, my dear Lady, your most obliged and affectionate friend,

Nelson & Bronte


I am told, the moment 'St George' arrives, that I am to be tumbled out of this ship; as the 'Ville de Paris' is going to Plymouth to be paid, and the Earl will hoist his flag here; and if I am as fortunate in getting a fresh painted cabin (which is probable) I shall be knocked up. At all events, I shall be made very uncomfortable by this hurry.

It has been very good, and friendly, of Mr Davidson, to travel upwards of two hundred miles, to make me a visit.

I rather think, the great Earl will not much like his not having called on him; but his manner of speaking to Mr Davidson, for his friendship to me, in the manner of a law-suit, Lord St Vincent states to my solicitors as offensive to him. Why should it? only that Mr Davidson wishes that I should have justice done me, and not to be over-powered by weight of interest and money.

Once more, god bless you and Sir William,

N & B


Sir Isaac Heard has gazetted Troubridge's, Hood, and etc's honours; but has not gazetted mine: and he has the King's orders for mine as much as the others.

San Josef
February 16th, 1801

My Dearest Friend,

Your letters have made me happy, today; and never again will I scold unless you begin. Therefore pray, never do; my confidence in you is firm as a rock.

I cannot imagine, who could have stopped my Sunday's letter! That it has been is clear: and the seal of the other has been clearly opened: but might have happened from letters sticking together.

Yours all came safe; but the numbering of them will point out, directly, if one is missing. I do not think,, that anything particular was in that letter which is lost.

Believe me, my dear friend, That Lady A. is as damned a w..... as ever lived, and Mrs M---- is a bawd! Mrs U---- a foolish pimp; eat up with pride, that a P---- will condescend to put her to expence. Only do as I do; and all will be well, and you will be everything I wish.

I thank you for your kindness to poor Mrs Thompson. I send her a note; as desired by her dear good friend, who doats on her.

I send you a few lines, wrote in the late gale: which I think, you will not disapprove.

How interesting your letters are! you cannot write too much, or be too particular.

Though --------'s polish'd verse superior shine,
Though sensibility grace every line;
Though her soft Muse be far above all praise,
And female tenderness inspire her lays:

Deign to receive, though unadorn'd
By the poetic art,
The rude expressions which bespeak
A sailor's untaught heart!

A heart susceptible, sincere, and true;
A heart, by fate, and nature, torn in two:
One half to duty and his country due;
The other, better half, to love and you!

26

Sooner shall Britain's sons resign
The empire of the sea;
Than Henry shall renounce his faith,
And plighted vows, to thee!

And waves on waves shall cease to roll,
And tides forget to flow,
Ere thy true Henry's constant love,
Or ebb, or change, shall know.

The weather, thank God, is moderating. I have just got a letter from the new Earl at the Admiralty, full of compliments. But nothing shall stop my law-suit, and I hope to cast him.

I trust, when I get to Spithead, there will be no difficulty in getting leave of absence.

The letters on service are so numerous, from three days' interruption of the post, that I must conclude with assuring you, that I am for ever, your attached, and unalterably yours,

Nelson & Bronte

I shall begin a letter to-night.

Parting from such a friend is literally tearing one's own flesh; but the remembrance will keep up our spirits till we meet. My affection is, if possible, stronger than ever for you. And I trust it will keep increasing as long as we both live. I have seen Mrs Thompson's friend, who is delighted at my having seen his dear child. I am sure he will be very fond of it. I arrived hear before noon, and have had my hands full of business.

Tomorrow we embark troops, I will write you a long letter tonight, and send it under cover to Troubridge; therefore you will have on Sunday. For ever, aye for ever, believe me, &c.

Hardy, Parker, and Freemantle, desire their remembrances.


'San Josef'


Mrs Thompson, to the care of Lady Hamilton


I gave your letter to your friend, who is much pleased with your resolution. He says he feels confident of your conduct, and begs you will follow the admirable conduct of our dear Lady Hamilton, who will send the Prince to the devil. He again begs me to be his bondsman, and that he will marry you the moment your uncle dies or it comes a peace, and he desires his blessings to his child, and you will forgive my desiring you to kiss it for me. Your friend has not been very well, but hopes to be better very soon. Ever believe me, your & his sincere friend.

After my letter of 8 o'clock this morning went on shore, on board came Oliver, and when he was announced by Hardy, so much anxiety for your safety rushed into my mind that a pain immediately seized my heart which kept increasing for half an hour, that, turning cold, hot, cold, &c., I was obliged to send for the surgeon, who gave me something to warm me, for it was a deadly chill. This morning has brought me your three dear letters by the post, and as many from Troubridge. Parker being appointed to a fine ship, I have charged him to deliver into your own hands, if possible, this letter. Oliver I shall keep till tomorrow.

Why, my dear friend do you alarm yourself? Your own Nelson will return safe, and, under the hand of Providence, is as safe as if walking London streets. The troops are only 800, and are intended for the better manning of our ships. Recollect the more force we have the less risk. You may rely we shall return in May — perhaps long before; the sooner we are off, the quicker we return, and the enemy much less prepared to receive us. I wish it was in my power to get leave of absence for James Dugdale, but not even an ad. or captain could get an hour's leave and Sir Thomas Pasley at Plymouth has no power to grant it.

Amongst many cards, I think I saw somebody's rout, but as I cared for no rout, or the writers, I did not trouble my head about it. I am sure neither of us should have gone to Lady D's rout; we could have amused ourselves better at home. Mr Levington served that fellow right, damn him. That Lady Aber. is a damned bitch; she would pimp for her husband that she might get at her lovers, for I daresay no one satisfies her, but no proper lover but two that I know of. Would to God I had dined alone with you. What a desert we would have had. The time will come, and believe me, that I am, for ever, for ever your own.

Thanks for the account of my godchild. Heavens bless it! Our activity will make a peace, and then I would not call the King my uncle.

Sir Charles Sexton, the Commissioner, who you and Sir William would have known had you come to Portsmouth, is on board seeing the ship; he is charmed with your picture, and says he did not believe such a handsome woman existed. I told him your equal did not, and your goodness, abilities, and virtues exceeded far away your beauty.

He is a rough sailor, 70, and a very old friend of mine. He quite regrets you and Sir William did not come to Portsmouth with me.

Now, my dear wife, for such you are in my eyes and in the face of heaven, I can give full scope to my feelings, for I daresay Oliver will faithfully deliver this letter. You know, my dearest Emma, that there is nothing in this world that I would not do for us to live together, and to have our dear little child with us. I firmly believe that this campaign will give us peace, and then we will set off for Bronte. In twelve hours we shall be across the water and freed from all the nonsense of his friends, or rather pretended ones. Nothing but an event happening to him could prevent my going. And I am sure you will think so, for unless all matters accord it will bring 100 of tongues and slanderous reports if I separated from her (which I would do with pleasure the moment we can be united; I want to see her no more) therefore we must manage till we can quit this country or your uncle dies. I love, I never did love any one else. I never had a dear pledge of love till you gave me one, and you, thank my God, never gave one to any body else.

I think before March is out you will either see us back, or so victorious that we shall insure a glorious issue to our toils. Think what my Emma will feel at seeing return safe, perhaps with a little more fame, her own dear loving Nelson. Never, if I can help it, will I dine out of my ship, or go on shore, except duty calls me. Let Sir Hyde have any glory he can catch — I envy him not. You, my beloved Emma, and my country, are the two dearest objects of my fond heart — a heart susceptible and true. Only place confidence in me and you never shall be disappointed. I burn all your dear letters, because it is right for your sake, and I wish you would burn all mine — they can do no good, and will do us both harm if any seizure of them, or the dropping even one of them, would fill the mouths of the world sooner than we intend.

My longing for you, both person and conversation, you may readily imagine. What must be my sensations at the idea of sleeping with you! it sets me on fire, even the thoughts, much more would the reality. I am sure my love & desires are all to you, and if any woman naked were to come to me, even as I am this moment from thinking of you, I hope it might rot off if I would touch her even with my hand. No, my heart, person, and mind is in perfect union of love towards my own dear, beloved Emma — the real bosom friend of her, all hers, all Emma's, &c.

Oliver is gone to sleep, he is grown half foolish. I shall give him £10 in the morning, and I have wrote a letter recommending a friend of his to the Chairman of the East India Company, which he said you would be glad I should do for him. I have nothing to send my

Emma, it makes me sorry you & Sir Wm could not come to Yarmouth, that would be pleasant, but we shall not be there more than a week at farthest. I had a letter this day from the Rev. Mr. Holden, who we met on the

Continent; he desired his kind compliments to you and Sir William: he sent me letters of my name, and recommended it as my motto — Honor est a Nilo — Horatio Nelson. May the Heavens bless you. (My love, my darling angel, my heaven-given wife, the dearest only true wife of her own till death, &c. I know you will never let that fellow or any one come near you.)

Monday Morning — Oliver is just going on shore; the time will ere long arrive when Nelson will land to fly to his Emma, to be for ever with her. Let that hope keep us up under our present difficulties. Kiss and bless our dear Horatia — think of that.

Having, my truly Dearest Friend, got through a great deal of business, I am enabled to do justice to my private feelings; which are fixed, ever, on you, and about you, whenever the public service does not arrest my attention.

I have read all, all, your kind and affectionate letters: and have read frequently over: and committed them to the flames much against my inclinations.

There was one I rejoiced not to have read at the time. It was where you consented to dine and sing with....... Thank God, it was not so! I could not have borne it; and now, less than ever. But, I now know, he never can dine with you; for, you would go out of the house sooner than suffer it: and, as to letting him hear you sing, I only hope he will be struck deaf, and you dumb, sooner than such a thing should happen! But, I know, it never now can.

You cannot think how my feelings are alive towards you, probably more than ever: and they never can be diminished. My hearty endeavours shall not be wanting, to improve and to <u>give us new</u> ties of regard and affection.

I have seen, and talked much with, Mrs Thompson's friend. The fellow seems to eat all my words, when I talk of her and his child. He says, he never can forget our goodness and kind affection to her and his dear, dear child, I have had, you know, the felicity of seeing it, and a finer child never was produced by any two persons.

It was, in truth, a love be-gotten child! I am determined to keep him on board; for, I know, if they got together, they would soon have another. But, after our two months trip, I hope, they will never be separated; and, then, let them do as they please.

We are all bustle and activity. I shall sail on Monday, after your letter arrives. Troubridge will send it, as an Admiralty letter. On Tuesday I shall be in the Downs, if they have any wind: and Troubridge will send, under cover to Admiral Lutwidge.

It is not my intention to set my foot out of the ship, except to make my take-leave bow to Admiral Milbank. I have been much pressed to dine ashore, but, no; never, if I can help it, till I dine with you.

*Eleven o'clock.*

*Your dear letters just come on board. They are sympathetic with my own feelings; and, I trust, we shall soon meet to part no more!*

*Monday, I shall be here for letters; Tuesday, at Deal. Recollect, I am, for ever, yours; aye, for ever, while life remains, yours, yours faithfully,*

*Nelson & Bronte*

*I charge my only friend to keep well, and think of her Nelsons glory.*

*I have written to Lord Eldon, the Chancellor, as my brother desired.*

*Pray, as you are going to buy a ticket for the Pigot diamond — buy the right number, or it will be money thrown away.*

*For ever, ever, yours and only yours. Kindest regards to my dear Mrs Thompson, and my God Child.*

'St George' at Sea
March 6th 1801

How tiresome and alone I feel at not having the pleasure of receiving your dear, kind, friendly, and intelligent letters. I literally feel as a fish out of water. Calms and foul winds have already prolonged our passage from what is often done in fourteen hours to three days, and yet no appearance of our arrival this day.

It now snows and rains and is nearly calm. All day yesterday I was employed about a very necessary thing; and I assure you it gave me great pleasure, instead of pain, the reflection that I was providing for a great friend. I have given you, by will, £3000, and three diamond boxes, & the King of Naples picture in trust, to be at your disposal, so that it is absolutely your own. By the codicil I have given you the money owing to me by Sir William, likewise in trust. The trustees are, Mr Ryder, a very eminent law man, and Mr Davidson; they will be my executors.

I you like any body else, say so, and it shall be done. The star I have given you to wear for my sake. You must not think my dearest friend, that this necessary act hastens our departure, but it is a right and proper measure. (Why should my friends be neglected, and those who I care nothing for have my little fortune, which I have worked so hard and I think so honourably for?)

Half past eight, - Just anchored in the sea, thick as mud. I am really miserable; I look at all your pictures, at your dear hair, I am ready to cry, my heart is so full. Then I think you may see that fellow.

I shall never forgive it. It would go near to kill me; but I never will believe it till I know it for certain.

Noon. — Under sale, steering for Yarmouth, but cannot arrive before 5 o'clock. How I regret not being in time to save the post, for I judge as of my own fleet.

Three o'clock. — In sight of Yarmouth. With what different sensations to what I saw it before! Then I was with all I hold dear in the world; now, unless the pleasure I shall have in reading your dear, dear letters, how different to the approach. Although we are to late for the post, yet Hardy will take this letter on shore. I shall put it under cover for Troubridge as I shall those of tomorrow.

May the Heavens bless my own dear friend and let me read happy and good news from her. Kiss my dear, dear godchild for me, and be assured I am for ever, ever, ever, your, your, your, more than ever yours, your own, only your, &c.

I am wet through and cold.

Deal — (Shall be on board 'Medusa'
before this letter go from the Downs)
July 31, 1801

My Dearest Emma,

Did not you get my letter from Sheerness on Thursday morning, telling you I was just setting off for Deal: as I have no letter from you yesterday, only those of Wednesday which went to Sheerness?

It has been my damned blunder, and not yours; for which I am deservedly punished by missing one of your dear letters. They are my comfort, joy, and delight.

My time is truly, fully taken up, and my hand aches before night comes. I got to bed, last night, at half past nine; but the hour was so unusual that I heard the clock strike one. To say that I thought of you, would be nonsense; for, you are never out of my thoughts.

At this moment, I see no prospect of my getting to London; but, very soon the business of my command will become so simple, that a child may direct it.

What rascals your post-chaise people must be! They have been paid everything. Captain Parker has one receipt for seven pounds odd, and I am sure that everything is paid, therefore, do not pay a farthing. The cart-chaise I paid at Dartford.

You need not fear all the women in this world: for all others, except your-self, are pests to me. I know but one; for, who can be like my Emma? I am confident, you will do nothing which will hurt my feelings; and I will die by torture, sooner than anything which could offend you. Give ten thousand kisses to my dear Horatia.

Yesterday, the subject turned on the cow-pox. A gentleman declared, that his child was inoculated with the cow-pox; and afterwards remained in a house where a child had the cow-pox the natural way, and did <u>not</u> catch it. Therefore, here was a full trial with the cow-pox. The child is only feverish for two days; and only a slight inflammation of the arm takes place, instead of being all over scabs. But do you what you please.

I do not get your newspapers; therefore, do not know what promise you allude to, but this I know, I have <u>none</u> made me.

The extension of the patent of peerage is going on: but the wording of my brother's note, they have wrote for a meaning to. The patent must be a new creation. First, to my father, if he outlives me: then to William and his sons; then to Mrs Bolton, and her sons: and Mrs Matcham, and hers. Farther than that I care not; it is far enough. But it may never get to any of them; for the old patent may extend by issue male of my own carcase. I am not very old: and may marry again, a wife more suitable to my genius.

I like the 'Morning Chronicle'. Ever, for ever, yours, only your

## Nelson & Bronte

Best regards to Mrs Nelson, the Duke, and Lord William.
I have totally failed for poor Madame Brueys.
Bonaparte's wife is one of Martinique, and some plan is supposed to be carried on.

Sheerness
August 11th, 1801

My Dearest Emma,

I came from Harwich yesterday noon; not having set my foot on shore, although the Volunteers, etc., were drawn up to receive me, and the people ready to draw the carriage.

Parker had very near got all the honours; but I want none, but what my dear Emma confers. You have sense to discriminate whether they are deserved or no.

I came on shore: for my business lays with the Admiral, who lives on a ship hauled on shore, and the Commissioner. Slept at Coffin's, and, having done all that I can, am off for the Downs; today if possible.

As far as September 14th, I am at the Admiralty's disposal; but, if Mr Buonaparte do not chuse to send his miscreants before that time my health will not bear me through equinoctial gales.

I wish that Sir William was returned, I would try to persuade him to come to either Deal, Dover, or Margate: for, thus cut off from the society of my dearest friends, 'tis but a life of sorrow and sadness. But, 'patienza per forza!'

I hope you will get the house. If I buy, no person can say — this shall, or not be altered: and, you shall have the whole arrangements.

Remember me most kindly to Mrs Nelson, the Duke, and Lord William.

Write to me in the Downs. May the Heavens bless and preserve you, for ever and ever! is the constant prayer of, my dear Emma, your most affectionate and faithful

*Nelson & Bronte*

The Mayor and Corporation of Sandwich, when they came on board to present me the freedom of that ancient town, requested me to dine with them.

I put them off for the moment, but they would not let me off. Therefore this business, dreadful to me, stands over, and I shall be attacked again when I get to the Downs. But I will not dine there, without you say, approve: nor, perhaps, then, if I can get off. Oh! how I hate to be stared at.

Deal, August 18th 1801

My Dearest Emma,

Your dear, good, kind, and most affectionate letters, from Saturday to last night, are arrived, and I feel all you say: and may Heaven bless me, very soon, with a sight of your dear angelic face. You are a nonpareil! No, not one fit to wipe your shoes. I am, ever have been, and always will remain, your most firm, fixed, and unalterable friend.

I wish Sir William had come home a week ago, then I should have seen you here.

I have this morning been attending the funeral of two young mids., a Mr Gore, cousin of Capt. Gore, and a Mr Bristow. One nineteen, the other seventeen years of age.

Last night, I was all evening in the hospital, seeing that all was done for the comfort of the poor fellows.

I am going on board; for nothing should keep me living on shore, without you were here. I shall come in the morning, to see Parker, and go on board again directly.

I shall be glad to see Oliver. I hope he will keep his tongue quiet, about the tea kettle; for, I shall not give it till I leave the 'Medusa'.

You ask me what Troubridge wrote me? There was not a syllable about you in it. It was about my not coming to London; at the importance of which, I laughed and, then, he said, he should never venture another opinion. On which, I said —

"Then, I shall never give you one". This day, he has wrote a kind letter and all is over. I have, however, wrote him, in my letter of this day, as follows —

"And I am, this morning, as firmly of opinion as ever, that Lord Vincent and yourself, should have allowed of my coming to town, for my own affairs; for, every one knows, I left it without a thought for myself".

I know, he likes to be with you: but, shall he have that felicity, and <u>he</u> deprive me of it? No; that he shall not!

But this business cannot last long, and I hope we shall have peace; and I rather incline to that opinion. But the Devil should not get out of the kingdom, without being some days with you.

I hope, my dear Emma, you will be able to find a house suited for my comfort.

I am sure of being <u>happy</u>, by your arrangements .

I have wrote a line to Troubridge, about Darby. Parker will write you a line of thanks, if he is able. I trust in God, he will yet do well!

You ask me, my dear friend, if I am going on more expeditions? And, even if I was to forfeit your friendship, which is dearer to me than all the world, I can tell you nothing.

For, I go out; if I see the enemy and can get at them, it is my duty and you would naturally hate me, if I kept back one moment.

I long to pay them for their tricks t'other day, the debt of a drubbing, which, surely, I'll pay: but <u>when</u>, <u>where</u>, or <u>how</u>, it is impossible, your own good sense must tell you, for me or mortal man to say.

I shall not act in a rash or hasty manner; that you may rely, and on which I give you my word of honour.

Just going off. Ever, for ever, your faithful

*Nelson & Bronte*

Every kind thing to Mrs Nelson.

My Dear Emma, Dearest, Best, Friend of Nelson,

Sir William is arrived, and well; remember me kindly to him. I should have had the pleasure of seeing him, but for one of my 'lords and masters,' Troubridge; therefore I am sure, neither you or Sir William will feel obliged to him.

The weather is very bad, and I am very sea-sick. I cannot answer your letter, probably; but I am a writing line, to get on shore, if possible; indeed I hardly expect that your letter can get afloat.

I entreat you, my dear friend, to work hard for, and to get the house and furniture; and I will be so happy to lend it to you and Sir William.

Therefore if you was to take the Duke's house, 'a cake house', open to everyone he pleases, you had better have a book at once; you never could rest one moment quiet. Why did not the Duke assist Sir William when he wanted his assistance? Why not have saved you from the distress, which Sir William must every day feel, in knowing that his excellent wife sold her jewels to get a house for him; whilst her own relations, great as they are in the foolish world's eye, would have left a man of his respectability and age to have lodged in the streets. Did the Duke, or any of them, give him a house <u>then</u>? Forgive me! you know if anything sticks in my throat, it must be out. Sir William owes his life to you; which I believe he will never forget.

To return to the house — the furniture must be bought with it; and the sooner it is done the better I shall like it.

Oh! how bad the weather is!

The devils, here, wanted to plague my soul out, yesterday, just after dinner; but I would have seen them damned, before they should have come in.

The Countess Mountmorris, Lady this, that, and t'other, came alongside, a Mr Lubbock with them — to desire they might come in. I sent word, I was so busy that no person could be admitted, as my time was employed in the Kings service. Then they sent their names, which I cared not for; and sent Captain Gore, to say it is impossible; and that if they wanted to see a ship, they had better go to the 'Overyssel' (a sixty four in the Downs). They said, no; they wanted to see me. However, I was stout, and will not be shown about like a <u>beast</u>! - and away they went.

I believe, Captain Gore wishes me out of his ship; for the ladies admire him, I am told, very much; but however, no captain could be kinder to me than he is. These ladies he told me afterwards, were his relations.

I have just got your letters; many thanks, for them! You do not say, in the end, Sir William is arrived.

I am glad that you approve. You may rely, my dear friend, that I will not run any unnecessary risk! No more boat work I promise you; but, ever, your attached and faithful

*Nelson & Bronte*

To the Duke and Sir William, say everything which is kind; and to Mrs Nelson. I am so dreadfully sea-sick, that I cannot hold up my head!

September 21st, 1801
Quarter past ten o'clock

My Dear Emma,

I wish you would send the letter to Mrs Dod's, directly; for otherwise he may, inadvertently.

If done, and it comes to London, deliver some of the things. The wardrobe is hers; and if any of her clothes are at Mr Dod's, they had better be separated from mine — and indeed what things are worth removing — to have them directly sent to Merton. A bed or two, I believe belong to my father; but am not sure.

I send you Dr Bairds comfortable note, the moment received.

You will find Parker is treated like an infant. Poor fellow! I trust he will get well, and take possession of his room at the farm. Ever your affectionate,

*Nelson & Bronte*

My Dearest Emma,

Your kind letters came on board about six o'clock.

You may rely upon one thing, that I shall like Merton; therefore, do not be uneasy on that account. I have that opinion of your taste and judgement, that I do not believe it can fail in pleasing me. We must only consider our means; and for the rest, I am sure, you will soon make it the prettiest place in the world.

I dare say, Mr Hazelwood acted, like all lawyers, whose only consideration was for their client; but, I am sure, you will do, for me, all the civil things towards Mrs Greaves.

If I can afford to buy the Duck Close, and the adjoining field, it would be pleasant; but, I fear, it is not in my power: but, I shall know, when my accounts are settled, at New Year's Day.

To be sure, we will employ the trades-people of our village in preference to any others, in what we want for common use, and give them every encouragement to be kind and attentive to us. From my heart, do I wish that I was with you: and it cannot be long; for, today, I am far from well; violent headache, and very cold; but it may be agitation.

Whatever, my dear Emma, you do for my little charge, I must be pleased with.

Probably, she will be lodged at Merton; at least, in the spring, when she can have the benefit of our walks. It will make the poor mother happy, I am sure.

I do not write to her today, as this goes through the Admiralty; but tell her all I would say. You know my unchangeable thoughts about her.

I shall have the child christened, when I come up.

Have we a nice church at Merton? We will set an example of goodness to the under-parishioners.

Would to God, I was with you at Laleham. I shall never forget our happiness at that place. Mr Davidson will pay Mrs Nelson fifty pounds, October 1st. I dare say, Mr Shakespeare has some orders about it.

I had, yesterday, a letter from father; he seems to think that he may do something which I do not like. I suppose, he means, going to Somerset Street.

Shall I, to an old man, enter upon the detestable subject; it may shorten his days. But, I think, I shall tell him, that I cannot go to Somerset Street to see him. But, I shall not write till I hear your opinion.

If I once begin, you know, it will be all out, about her, and her ill-treatment to her son.

But, you shall decide.

Our accounts of dear Parker, I fear preclude all hopes of his recovery.

It was my intention to have gone ashore this morning, to have called on Admiral Lutwidge:

But, the wind's coming fresh from the S.W. I have declined it; I doubt, if I could get off again.

At ten o'clock, with your letters, came off Dr. Baird's note, to say every hope was gone! I have desired, that his death should be sent, by telegraph, to the Admiralty. They will, surely, honour his memory, although they would not promote him.

What are our feelings, my dear Emma! but, we must cheer up: and, with best regards to Mrs Nelson believe me ever, for ever, your most affectionate

*Nelson & Bronte*

Best regards to Sir William, I send you the last report. Who knows!

"Amazon", October 8, 1801.

My Dearest Friend,

I do not expect, although I am writing, that any boat can communicate with us today.

What can be the use of keeping me here? for, I can know nothing in such weather; and what a change since yesterday! It came on, in one hour, from the water like a mill-head, to such a sea as to make me very unwell. If I had gone to make any visit, I could not have got off again. I rejoice that I did not go.

Until I leave the station, I have no desire to go on shore, for Deal was always my abhorrence.

That Parker is a swindler. Langford owed our dear Parker twenty five pounds, of which there was no account; but Langford desired his agents to pay Mr Parker. Langford requested, that he would wait two or three months, as it would be more convenient to him. To which the other agreed — "Aye as long as you please". He got one pound, eleven shillings and sixpence from Samuel; by casting his account wrong. The first thing he does, is to desire Langford's agents to pay thirty four pounds for Langford, nine pounds more than the debt. He is worse than a public thief. His conduct to me was, absolutely the worst species of thieving; for, it was under false pretences. He sent Dr Baird on board, to me, to say, that in London, his pocket book was stole, in which was twenty pounds; and begged my assistance to get him home; and that he had not a farthing to buy mourning for his dear son. At this time he had forty-seven pounds in his pocket, beside what he had sold of his son's. He has behaved so unlike a gentleman, but very like a blackguard, to both Captain Sutton, Bedford, and Hardy, I am now clear that he never lost one farthing, and that the whole is a swindling trick.

So, you see, my dear friend, how good nature is imposed upon. I am so vexed that he should have belonged to our dear Parker!

I have now done with the wretch, for ever. I hope he has got nothing from you; and, if you have promised him anything, <u>do not send it</u>.

Ten o'clock

Your kind letters are arrived. I rejoiced that you have got into Merton. I hope to get the letter on shore; but it is very uncertain.

Ministry, my dearest friend, think very differently of my services from you!

But, never mind; I shall soon have done with them afloat.

Make my kindest regards to Sir William; and all our friends; and believe me ever, your faithful and affectionate

Nelson & Bronte

I have just got a very kind letter from Captain Read. He says, he will come and see me, be where it will. He enquired after you and Sir William.

My Dearest Friend,

This being a very fine morning, and smooth beach, at eight o'clock, I went with Sutton and Bedford, and landed at Walmer; but found Billy fast asleep; so, left my card; walked the same road that we came, when the carriage could not come with us that night; and all rushed into my mind, and brought tears into my eyes. Ah! how different to walking with such a friend as you, and Sir William and Mrs Nelson.

Called at the barracks, on Lord George; but he is gone to London.

From thence to the Admiral's, found him up; and, waiting half an hour to see Mrs Lutwidge; who has been worse these few days past, and God knows when he will be well. I am afraid it will be a long time; for several pieces of bone are lately come away, and more to come.

But Troubridge has so completely prevented my ever mentioning anybody's service, that I am become a cypher, and he has gained a victory over Nelson's spirit. I am kept here; for what, he may be able to tell, I cannot; but long it cannot, shall not, be.

Sutton and Bedford are gone a tour, till dinner-time: but nothing shall make me, but almost force, go out of the ship again, till I have done; and the Admiralty, in charity will be pleased to release me.

I am, in truth, not very well. I have a complaint in my stomach and bowels, but it will go off. If you was hear I should have some rhubarb; but as you are not, I shall go without.

Sutton has sent into Yorkshire, for a cow that, in the spring, will give fourteen pounds of butter a week; and, he has given Allen the finest goat I ever saw. The latter, I am afraid, will be troublesome.

Just as I was coming off, I received your packet; and thank you, from my heart, for all your kindness.

What can Reverend Sir want to be made a doctor for? He will be laughed at for his pains!

I thank you for the King's letters. I shall write a kind line to Castelcicala, and answer the King's very soon; and, write to Acton; for he can make Bronte everything to me, if he pleases. I daresay, I did wrong, never to write to him; but as he treated Sir William unkindly, I never could bring myself to it.

I am glad the Duke has been to see you; and taking plants from him, is nothing. Make my kindest remembrances to him.

I would have everybody like your choice; for I am sure, you have as fine a taste in laying out land, as you have in music. I'll be damned, if Mrs Billington can sing so well as you. She may have stage trick, but you have pure nature.

I always say everything for you and Sir William. I wish you had translated the King's and Acton's letters, Banti cannot.

I may be able to dispose of Charles, but not of the other, and he would corrupt Charles. For ever yours

## Nelson & Bronte

Mrs Lutwidge inquires always particularly after you. We all laugh, and say she is more fond of soldiers than ever, since General Don has shewn her how he would keep off the French!

My Dearest Friend,

I have received all your letters of yesterday, and the one sent from the post at Merton; and, also, one mis-sent to Poole; but I do not write direct to Merton, till I hear that mine to Sir William, sent yesterday, gets to you before those by London.

The Admiralty will not give me leave, till the 22nd; and, then, only ten days. What a set of beasts!

My cold is now got into my head; and I have such dreadful pain in my teeth that I cannot hold up my head; but none of them cares a damn for me or my sufferings; therefore, you see, I cannot discharge my steward.

And, yet, I think upon consideration, that I will send up all my things, and take my chance as to their sending me down again. What do you think?

At all events, everything except my bed. I have tablespoons, forks, everything; at least, I shall have, soon, two hundred pounds worth.

What a b----- that Miss Knight is! As to the other, I care not what she says.

My poor dear father is wrong. But more of this, when we meet: which will be Friday, the 23rd at farthest; if possible, the 22nd. But the Admiralty are hard on me.

I am sorry to hear, that you have been ill; and my cold is so dreadfully bad; that I cannot hold up my head; and am so damned stupid that you must, my dear friend, forgive my letter.

Admiral Lutwidge is going to Portsmouth. Sir William Parker is going to be tried for something. Make my kindest respects to Sir William; and believe me, ever, yours most faithfully,

*Nelson & Bronte*

I have wrote a line to Merton. Excuse my letter.

My Dearest Friend,

It being a very fine morning, and the beach smooth, I went to call upon Admiral Lutwidge, and returned on board before ten o'clock.

Mrs Lutwidge is delighted with your present. Sutton,etc., were called forth to admire it. She joins in abusing the Admiralty. She pressed me very much to dine with them at three o'clock; but I told her I would not dine with the angel Gabriel, to be dragged through a night surf! Her answer was, that she hoped soon I should dine with an angel, for she was sure you was one. In short, she adores you; but, who does not? You are so good, so kind, to everybody; old, young, rich, or poor, it is the same thing!

I called upon poor Langford; who has a long time to look forward to for getting well; he told me your goodness, in writing him a line; and I called upon Dr Baird; he disapproves of rhubarb, and has prescribed magnesia and peppermint; and I called on Mr Lawrence. So, you see, I did much business in one hour I was on shore. Civility to Lutwidge was proper for me; and, indeed, my duty.

The moment I got your letters, off I came, and have read them with pleasure. They have made me much better, I think; at least, I feel so.

I admire the pigs and poultry. Sheep are certainly most beneficial to eat off the grass. Do you get paid for them; and take care that they are kept on the premises all night, for that is the time they do good to the land. They should be folded. Is your head man a good person, and true to our interest? I intend to have a farming book. I am glad to hear you get fish; not very good ones, I fancy.

It is, I thank God, only six days before I shall be with you, and to be shewn all the beauties of Merton. I shall like it, leaves or no leaves.

No person there can take amiss our not visiting. The answer from me will always be very civil thanks, but that I wish to live retired. We shall have our sea friends; and I know, Sir William thinks they are the best.

I have a letter from Mr Trevor, begging me to recommend a youngster for him; but none before your Charles. Banti, I suppose, must return; but, at present, we know not what ships are to be kept in commission.

I have a letter from a female relation of mine. She has had three husbands; and he, Mr Sherstone, three wives. Her brother, a Nelson, I have been trying, ever since I have been in England, to get promoted. The last and present Admiralty promised. I never saw the man;

he is on a ship in the North Seas, forty five years of age.

I have a letter from Troubridge; recommending me to wear flannel shirts. Does he care for me? No; but never mind. They shall work hard, to get me back again.

Remember me, kindly, to Sir William, the Duke, and all friends; and believe me, ever, your most affectionate

*Nelson & Bronte*

Do you ever see Castelcicala? He is a good man, and faithful to his master and mistress.

"Amazon", October 16th, 1801

My Dearest Friend,

I send you a letter for Allen's wife; and one for Germany, which I wish you would make Oliver put in the Foreign Post Office, and pay what is necessary.

I would send you the letter to which it is an answer, but it would be an overweight. It is all compliments; and the man says it is all truth.

The wind is freshened cold, but very fine day.

Best regards to Sir William, Mrs Cadogan, Mr Oliver, and all friends.

For ever, yours faithfully,

*Nelson & Bronte*

I have a letter from Reverend Doctor — he is as big as if he was a Bishop; and one from the Bedel of the university, to say how well he preached. I hope you ordered something good for him, for those big wigs love eating and drinking.

My Dearest Friend,

Although my complaint has no danger of attending it, yet it resists the medicines that Dr Baird has prescribed; and, I fancy, it has pulled me down very much.

The cold has settled in my bowels. I wish the Admiralty had my complaint: but, they have no bowels; at least for me.

I had a very indifferent night, but you and Sir William's kind letters have made me feel better.

I send you a letter from Lord Pelham. I shall certainly attend: and let them see, that I may be useful in council, as I have been in the field. We must submit; and perhaps those Admiralty do this by me, to prevent another application.

You may rely, that I shall be with you by dinner, on Friday; at half past three or four at the farthest.

I shall not dine with Pitt, as Mr and Mrs Long are staying there. Not that I ever saw her in my life, nor care if I never do.

I pray that I will not be annoyed, on my arrival: it is retirement with my friends, that I wish for.

Thank Sir William, kindly, for his letter; and the enclosure, which I return.

Sutton is much pleased with your letter; and, with Bedford, will certainly make you a visit. They are both truly good and kind to me.

Our weather has been cold these two days, but not bad. I have got a fire in the cabin, and, I hope, my complaint may go off.

May Heaven bless you! I send this, through Troubridge, direct in Piccadilly.

I shall, you may rely, admire the pig-stye, ducks, fowls, etc., for everything you do, I look upon as perfect.

Dr Baird has been on board, to see me. He thinks, I shall be better; and, that a few days on shore will set me up again.

Make my kind remembrances to Sir William, the Duke, and all friends; and believe me, ever, your most affectionate

*Nelson & Bronte*

Bedford has made me laugh. Mrs Lutwidge has been babbling, that she will go to

Portsmouth with the Admiral, who says, he shall be so fully employed, that he cannot be much with her. She whispered to Bedford — " I have many friends in the army there!" She will certainly marry a soldier, if ever she is disposable.     But perhaps, you will agree with me, that no good soldier would take her.  I am sure, the purchase would be dear, even if it was a gift.  Don't call this a bull.

Sutton's man was on the farm; and the sheep, when not belonging to the farm always paid so much sheep, so much lambs: but, I dare say, you manage well.

Sir William's letter has delighted me, with your activity and prudence.


Oct. 1801


My Dearest Friend,
    Hardy begs you will send the inclosed to Naples.
I wish Tyson would come home; for many are pulling at him, and I want to pay him.  I will not be in his debt forty-eight hours after his arrival.
Hardy is just anchored, and his commodore gone on shore.
Ever your most faithful


Nelson & Bronte


Mrs Nelson had better direct her letters to me unless I am on the spot.  You see, you paid postage, and it lays me open to their Post Office conversation.

My Dearest Friend,

What a gale we have had! But Admiral Lutwidge's boat came off; and, as your letter was wrote, it got on shore; at least, I hope so; for the boat seemed absolutely swallowed up in the sea. None of our boats could have kept above water a moment; therefore, I could not answer all the truly friendly things you told me in your letters, for they were not opened before the boat was gone.

I am sure, you did well to send Mrs Lutwidge a gown, and she loves you very much, but there is no accounting for taste. She admires entirely red coats; you, true blue.

They dine with Billy Pitt, today: or rather with Mr Long; for Pitt does not keep house, in appearance, although he asked me to come and see him: and that I shall do, out of respect to a great man, although he never did anything for me or my relations.

I assure you, my dear friend, that I had rather read and hear all your little story of a white hen getting into a tree, an anecdote of Fatina, or hear you call — "Cupidity! Cupidity!" than any speech I shall hear in parliament; because I know, although you can adapt your language and manners to a child, yet that you can also thunder forth such a torrent of eloquence, that corruption and infamy would sink before your voice, in however exalted a situation it might be placed.

Poor Oliver! what can be the matter with him?

I must leave my cot here, till my discharge, when it shall come to the farm, as cots are the best things in the world for our sea friends.

Why not have the pictures from Davison's, and those from Dodd's: especially my father's and Davison's.

Apropos! Sir William has not sat, I fear to Beechey — I want a half length the size of my father's and Davison's.

I wonder your pictures are not come from Hamburg! You have not lost the directions for unfolding them; nor the measure, that I may have frames made for them? For, up they shall go, as soon as they arrive. What, have your picture, and not hang it up! No: I will submit, in the farm, to every order but <u>that</u>.

The weather, today, is tolerable; but I do not think I could well get on shore; but Thursday, I hope, will be a fine day.

I shall call on Mr Pitt, make my visit at the hospital, and get off very early on Friday morning.

My cold is still very troublesome, I cannot get my bowels in order. In the night I had not a little fever. But, never mind: the Admiralty will not always be there. Everyone has their day.

God bless you, my dear friend; and believe me, ever, yours most faithfully,

Nelson & Bronte

Write on Wednesday.

Your letters of yesterday are received. Reverend Doctor would like to be a Bishop. I have sent poor Thomson's letter, and the distressed Mrs------ to the Earl. Kindest regards to Sir William.

My Dearest Friend,

How could you think, for a moment, that I would be a time server to any Minister on earth! And, if you had studied my letter a little closer, you would have seen that my intention was, to shew them that I could be as useful in the cabinet as in the field.

My idea is, to let them see that my attendance is worth soliciting. For myself, I can have nothing, but, for my brother, something may be done.

Living with Mr Addington a good deal; never, in your sense of the word, shall I do it. What, leave my dearest friends, to dine with a minister? Damn me, if I do, beyond what you yourself shall judge to be necessary! Perhaps, it may be <u>once</u>; and <u>once</u> with the Earl, but that you shall judge for me. If I give up all intercourse — you know enough of Courts, that they will do nothing: make yourself of consequence to them, and they will do what you wish, in reason; and, out of reason, I never should ask them. It must be a great bore to me, to go to the House. I shall tell Mr Addington, that I go on the 29th to please him and not to please myself; but more of this subject, when we meet.

Dr Baird is laid up with rheumatism; he will now believe, that the cold may affect me. This is the coldest place in England, most assuredly.

Troubridge writes me that, as the weather is set in fine again, he hopes I shall get walks on shore. He is, I suppose, laughing at me; but never mind.

I agree with you, in wishing Sir William had a horse. Why don't you send to the Duke for a pony for him.

I am just parting with four of my ships — Captains Conn, Rowley, Martin and Whitter — who are proceeding to the Nore, in their way to be paid off.

The surf is so great on the beach, that I could not land dry, if it was necessary, today; but, I hope, it will be smooth on Thursday; if not, I must go in a boat to Dover, and come from thence to Deal.

Sutton says, he will get the "Amazon" under sail, and carry me down; for, that I shall not take cold; Bedford goes with a squad to Margate; so that all our party will be broke up. I am sure, to many of them, I feel truly obliged.

Make my kindest respects to Sir William; and believe me ever, your most faithful and affectionate

*Nelson & Bronte*

I wish Banti was separated from Charles, for he is a knowing one.

I wish I could get him with a good Captain, who would keep him strict to his duty. Hardy cannot get paid a hundred pounds he advanced for Mr William's nephew. Many thanks for Mrs Nelson's letters.

The Reverend Doctor likes going about. Only think of his wanting to come up with an address of thanks! Why the King will not receive him, although he is a doctor; and less, for being my brother — for, they certainly do not like me.

My Dearest Friend,

Only two days more, the Admiral could, with any conscience, keep me here; not that I think, they have had any conscience.

I daresay, Master Troubridge is grown fat. I know I am grown lean, with my complaint: which, but for their indifference about my health, would never have happened; or, at least, I should have got well, long ago, in a warm room, with a good fire, and sincere friends.

I believe, I leave this squadron with sincere regret, and with the good wishes of every creature in it.

How I should laugh, to see you, my dear friend, rowing in a boat; the beautiful Emma rowing a one armed admiral in a boat! It will certainly be caricatured.

Well done, farmer's wife! I'll bet your turkey against Mrs Nelson's; but Sir William and I will decide.

Hardy say's you may be sure of him; and, that he has not lost his appetite. You will make us rich, with your economy —

I did not think, tell Sir William, that impudence had got such a deep root in Wales. I send you the letter, as a curiosity; and to have the impudence to recommend a midshipman!

It is not long ago, a person from Yorkshire desired me to lend him three hundred pounds as he was going to set up a school!

Are these people mad; or, do they take me for quite a fool?

However, I have wisdom enough to laugh at their folly, and to be, myself, your most obliged and faithful friend,

*Nelson & Bronte*

My Dearest Friend,

It blows strong from the westward, and is a very dirty day, with a good deal of surf on the beach; but Hardy and Sutton recommended my going on shore this morning, as they believe it may blow a heavy gale to-morrow.

But, what comfort would I have had, for two whole days, at Deal?

I hope the morning will be fine: but I have ordered a Deal boat, as they understand the beach better than ours; and if I cannot land here, I shall go to Ramsgate pier, and come to Deal in a carriage.

Has Mrs Cadogan got my Peer's robe? for I must send for Mr Webb, and have it altered to a Viscount's.

Lord Hood wrote to me, to-day, as he is to be one of my introducers. He wanted me to dine with him on the 24th, but I'll be damned if I dine from home on that day, and it would be as likely we should dine out on the 23rd.

If you and Sir William ever wish me to dine with his brother, it must be the time of a very small party; for it would be worse than death to me, to dine in so large a party.

I expect, that all animals will increase where you are, for I never expect you will suffer any to be killed. I am glad Sir William has got the Duke's pony: riding will do him much good.

I am sorry to tell you, that Dr Baird is so ill, that I am told it is very probable he may never recover. This place is the devil's for dreadful colds; and I don't believe I should get well all the winter; for both cough, and bowels, are still very much out of order.

You are now writing your last letter for Deal; so am I, for Merton, from Deal; at least I hope so; for, if I can help it I will not return to it.

I have much to do, being the last day on board; but ever, my dearest friend, believe me, your truly affectionate

*Nelson & Bronte*

I am literally starving with cold; but my heart is warm. I suppose I shall dine with Lutwidge; but I am not very desirous of it; for I shall have Sutton, Bedford and Hardy, with me.

You must prepare Banti's mother, as it is a peace, for some other line of life than the Navy. Yesterday he sold a pair of silver buckles; he would soon ruin poor Charles, who is really a well-disposed boy.

I never shall get warm again, I believe. I cannot feel the pen.

Make my kindest regards to Sir William, Mrs Cadogan, Oliver, etc. Sutton, Hardy and Bedford, all join in kind remembrances.

As Monday is Horace's birthday I suppose I must send him a one pound note.

"Victory" May 20th 1803

You will believe that although I am glad to leave that horrid place Portsmouth, yet the being afloat makes me now feel that we do not tread the same element. I feel from my sole that God is good, and in His due wisdom will unite us, only when you look upon our dear child call to your remembrance all you think that I would say was I present, and be assured that I am thinking of you every moment. My heart is full to bursting! May God Almighty bless & protect you, is the fervent prayer of, my dear beloved Emma, your most faithful, affectionate & c.

My Dearest Emma,

We are now in sight of Ushant, and shall see Admiral Cornwallis in an hour.

I am not in a little fret, on the idea that he may keep the "Victory," and turn us all into the "Amphion". It will make it truly uncomfortable; but, I cannot help myself.

I assure you, my dear Emma, that I feel a thorough conviction, that we shall meet again, with honour, riches, and health, and remain together till a good old age.

I look at your, and my God's Child's picture; but till I am sure of remaining here, I cannot bring myself to hang them up. Be assured, that my attachment, and affectionate regard, is unalterable; nothing can shake it! And, pray, say so to my dear Mrs T. when you see her. Tell her that my love is unbounded, to her and her sweet child; and if she should have more, it will extend to all of them. In short, my dear Emma, say everything to her which your dear, affectionate heart and head can think of.

We are very comfortable, Mr Elliot is happy, has quite recovered his spirits; he was very low, at Portsmouth. George Elliot is very well; say so, to Lord Minto, Murrey, Sutton — in short, everybody in the ship, seems happy; and, if we should fall in with a French man-of-war, I have no fears but they will do as we used to do.

Hardy is gone into Plymouth, to see our Dutchman safe. I think she will turn out a good prize.

Gaetano desires his duty to Miledi! He is a good man; and, I daresay, will come back: for, I think, it cannot be a long war; just enough to make me independent in pecuniary matters.

If the wind stands, on Tuesday we shall be on the coast of Portugal; and, before next Sunday, in the Mediterranean. To Mrs Cadogan, say every kind thing; to good Mrs Nelson, the Doctor, etc., etc.,

If you like, you may tell them about the entailing of the pension: but, perhaps, he will be so taken up with Canterbury, that it will do for some dull evening at Hilborough.

I shall now stop, till I have on board the Admiral. Only, tell Mrs T. that I will write her the first safe opportunity. I am not sure of this.

I shall direct to Merton, after June 1st. Therefore as you change, make Davison take a direction to Nepean; but, I would not trouble him with too many directions, for fear of embroil.

We were close in with Brest, yesterday; and found, by a frigate, that Admiral Cornwallis had a rendezvous at sea. Thither we went; but to this hour, cannot find him. It blows strong. What wind we are losing!

If I cannot find the Admiral by six o'clock, we must all go into the "Amphion", and leave the "Victory," to my great mortification. So much for the wisdom of my superiors.

I keep my letter open to the last; for, I still hope; as I am sure, there is no good reason for my not going out in the "Victory".

I am just embarking in the " Amphion ": cannot find Admiral Cornwallis.

May God in Heaven bless you!  prays your most sincere

*Nelson & Bronte*

Stephens's publication I should like to have.
I have left my silver seal; at least I cannot find it.

My Dearest Emma,

Although I have wrote letters from various places, merely to say — "Here I am," and "There I am" — yet, as I have no doubt but that they would all be read, it was impossible for me to say more than — "Here I am, and well;" and I see no prospect of any certain mode of conveyance, but by sea; which with the means the Admiralty has given me of small vessels can be but seldom.

Our passages have been enormously long. From Gibralter to Malta we were eleven days; arriving the fifteenth in the evening, and sailing in the night of the sixteenth — and it was the twenty-sixth before we got off Capri; where I ordered the frigate, which carried Mr Elliot to Naples, to join me.

I send you copies of the King and Queen's letters. I am vexed, that she did not mention you! I can only account for it by hers being a political letter.

When I wrote to the Queen, I said —

"I left Lady Hamilton, the eighteenth of May; and so attached to your Majesty, that I am sure she would lay down her life to preserve yours. Your Majesty never had a more sincere, attached, and real friend than your dear Emma. You will be sorry to hear, that good Sir William did not leave her in such comfortable circumstances as his fortune would have allowed. He has given it amongst his relations. But she will do honour to his memory, although every one else of his friends call loudly against him on that account."

I trust, my dear Emma, she has wrote you. If she can forget Emma, I hope God will forget her! But you think, she never will, or can. Now is her time to shew it. You will only shew the King and Queen's letters to some few particular friends.

The King is very low; lives mostly at Belvidere. Mr Elliot had not seen either him or the Queen, from the seventeenth, the day of his arrival, to the twenty-first. On the next day, he was to be presented.

I have made up my mind, that it is part of the plan of that Corsican scoundrel, to conquer the kingdom of Naples. He has marched thirteen thousand men into the kingdom, on the Adriatic side; and he will take possession with as much show of right, of Gaeta and Naples; and, if the poor King remonstrates, or allows us to secure Sicily, he will call it war, and declare a conquest.

I have cautioned General Acton, not to risk the Royal Family too long; but Naples will be conquered, sooner or later, as it may suit Buonaparte's convenience. The Morea, and Egypt, are likewise in his eye. An army of full seventy thousand men are assembling in Italy.

Gibbs and Noble are gone to Malta. I am, you may believe, very anxious to get off Toulon to join the fleet. Sir Richard Bickerton went from off Naples the day I left Gibraltar.

We passed Monte Christo, Bastia, and Cape Corse, yesterday; and are now moving, slowly, direct for Toulon.

What force they have, I know not; indeed, I am totally ignorant: some say, nine sail of the line; some, seven, some five. If the former, they will come out; for we have only the same number, including sixty-fours, and very shortly manned.

However, I hope they will come out, and let us settle the matter. You know, I hate being kept in suspence.

July 8th

I left this hole, to put down what force the French have at Toulon. Seven sail of the line ready, five frigates, and six corvettes. One or two more in about a week.

We, today, eight sail of the line — tomorrow, seven, including two sixty-four gun ships.

You will readily believe, how rejoiced I shall be to get one of your dear excellent letters, that I may know everything which has passed since my absence.

I sincerely hope, that Mr Booth has settled all your accounts. Never mind, my dear Emma, a few hundred pounds; which is all the rigid gripe of the law, not justice, can wrest from you. I thank God, that you cannot want; ( although that is no good reason for its being taken from you:) whilst I have sixpence, you shall not want for five pence of it!

But you have bought your experience, that there is no friendship in money concerns, and your good sense will make you profit of it.

I hope, the minister has done something for you. But never mind, we can live upon bread and cheese.

Independence is a blessing: and, although I have not yet found out the way to get prize money — which has been taken, has run into our mouths — however, it must turn out very hard, if I cannot get enough to pay off my debts, and that will be no small comfort.

I have not mentioned my Bronte affairs to Acton as yet; but, if Naples remains much longer, I shall ask the question. But, I expect nothing from them. I believe, even Acton wishes himself well, and safely removed.

I think, from what I hear, that the King's spirits are so much depressed, that he will give up the reins of Naples, at least, to his son, and to retire to Sicily.

Sir William, you know, always thought that he would end his life so. Certainly, his situation must be heart-breaking.

Gaetano returned in the frigate. I believe, he saw enough of Naples. He carried his family money; and Mr Falconer (Gibbs being absent) will pay

Mr Greville's pension to Gaetano's family. I have now sent Gaetano to the post; and he desires, to present his duty; and to tell you, that Mr Ragland, from Sir William's death, will not pay any more pensions, without orders from Mr Greville.

Vincenzo has had none paid. He is very poor; keeps a shop. His son wanted, I find, to come in the frigate to me. I cannot afford to maintain him; therefore I shall give no encouragement. Old Antonio was allowed a carline a day; that is, now, not paid. Sabatello lives with Mr Elliot.

Nicolo, and Mary Antonio, have left Mr Gibbs, for some cause; Gaetano says, he believes for 'amore'. Francesca has two children living, and another coming. She lives the best amongst them, like 'gallant homme'

Pasqual lives with the Duke Montelione; and Joseph with the old Russian.

Your house is a hotel; the upper parts are kept for the Marquis, the owner.

Mr Elliot has taken the house of the Baille Franconi, on the Chaia.

Doctor Nudi inquired kindly after us: and all the women at Santa Lucia expected, when they saw Gaetano, that you was arrived.

Bread never was so dear; everything else is plenty. The wages not being raised, Gaetano says, the poor of England are a million times better off.

So much for Gaetano's news. He desires his duty to Signora Madre; and remembrances to Mary Ann, Fatima, etc.

July 8th

We joined, this morning, the fleet. The men in the ships are good; but the ships themselves are a little the worse for wear, and very short of their complements of men. We shall never be better; therefore let them come; the sooner, the better.

I shall write a line to the Duke, that he may see I do not forget my friends: and I rely, my dearest Emma, on your saying every kind thing, for me, to the Doctor, Mrs Nelson, Mrs Bolton, Mr and Mrs Matcham, Mrs Cadagon; whose kindness, and goodness, I shall never forget.

You will have the goodness to send the inclosed, as directed, and be assured that I am, to the last moment of my life, your most attached, faithful, and affectionate,

Nelson & Bronte

"Victory" Off Toulon
August 1, 1803

(I do not know that you will get this letter)

My Dearest Emma,

Your letter of May 31, which came under cover to Mr Noble, of Naples, inclosing Davison's correspondence with Plymouth, arrived by the 'Phoebe' two days ago: and this is the only scrap of a pen which has been received by any person in the fleet since we sailed from England.

You will readily conceive, my dear Emma, the sensations which the sight and reading even your few lines occasioned. They cannot be understood, but by those of such mutual and truly sincere attachment as yours and mine. Although you said little, I understand a great deal, and most heartily approve of your plans and society for next winter: and, next spring, I hope to be rich enough to begin the alterations at dear Merton. It will serve to amuse you; and, I am sure, that I shall admire all your alterations, even to planting a gooseberry bush.

Sutton joined me yesterday, and we are all got into the 'Victory': and, a few days will put us in order.

Everybody gives a very excellent character of Mr Chevalier, the servant recommended by Mr Davison; and I shall certainly live as frugal as my station will admit. I have known the pinch, and shall endeavour never to know it again.

I want to send two thousand one hundred pounds, to pay off Mrs Greaves, on October 1st. But, I have not received one farthing: but I hope to receive some soon. But Mr Haslewood promised to see this matter right for me.

Hardy is now busy, hanging up your and Horatia's picture; and I trust soon to see the other two safe arrived from the Exhibition. I want no others to ornament my cabin. I can contemplate them, and find new beauties every day, and I do not want anybody else.

You will not expect much news from us. We see nothing. I have great fear, that all Naples will fall into the hands of the French; and if Acton does not take care, Sicily also. However, I have given my final advice so fully and strongly that, let what will happen, they cannot blame me.

Captain Capel says, Mr Elliot cannot bear Naples. I have no doubt, but that is very different to your time.

The Queen, I fancy, by the seal, has sent a letter to Castelcicala; her letter to me is only thanks for my attention to the safety of the kingdom. If Dr Scott has time, and is able, he shall write a copy for you.

The King is very much retired. He would not see the French General, St Cyr; who came to Naples, to settle the contribution for the payment of the French army.

The Queen was ordered to give him and the French Minister a dinner, but the King staid at Belvidere. I think, he will give it up soon; and retire to Sicily, if the French will allow him.

Acton has never dared give Mr Elliot, or one Englishman, a dinner.

The fleet are ready to come forth, but, they will not come for the sake of fighting me. I have this day made George Elliot, post; Lieutenant Pettit, a master and commander; and Mr Hindmarsh, gunner's son, of the 'Bellerophon', who behaved so well this day five year, a Lieutenant.

I reckon to have lost two French seventy-fours, by my not coming out in the 'Victory'; but I hope they will come soon, with interest.

This goes to Gibralter, by Sutton in the 'Amphion'. I shall write the Doctor in a day or two. I see, by the French papers, that he has kissed hands.

With kindest regards to your good mother, and all at Merton, etc., etc., ever yours, most faithfully and affectionately,

Nelson & Bronte

My Dearest Emma,

I take the opportunity of Mr Acourt's going through Spain with Mr Elliot's dispatches for England, to send this letter: for I would not, for the world, miss any opportunity of sending you a line.

By Gibralter, I wrote you, as lately as the 4th: but all our ways of communicating with England, are very uncertain: and I believe, the Admiralty must have forgotten us; for, not a vessel of any kind or sort has joined us, since I left Spithead.

News, I absolutely am ignorant of, except, that a schooner, belonging to me, put her nose into Toulon, and four frigates popped out, and have taken her, and a transport loaded with water for the fleet. However I hope to have the opportunity, very soon, of paying them the debt, with interest.

Mr Acourt says, at Naples, they hope that the mediation of Russia will save them, but, I doubt, if Russia will go to war with the French for any kingdom and they, poor souls! relying on a broken reed will lose Sicily.

As for getting anything for Bronte I cannot expect it; for, the finances of Naples are worse than ever. Patienza however, I will —

I see, many Bishops are dead. Is my brother tired of Canterbury? I wish I could make him a Bishop. If you see him, or write, say that I have not ten minutes to send away Mr Acourt who cannot be detained.

I hope Lord St Vincent has sent out Sir William Bolton. As soon as I know who is first Lord, I will write him.

My Dear Lady Hamilton,

Your friend's godson arrived safe yesterday afternoon: and I shall, you know, always feel too happy in obeying your commands: for, you never ask favours, but for your friends.

In short, in every point of view, from Ambassatrice to the duties of domestic life, I never saw your equal!

That elegance of manners, accomplishments, and, above all, your goodness of heart, is unparalleled: and only believe, for ever and beyond it, your faithful and devoted,

*Nelson & Bronte*

August 26th, 1803
Wrote several days past

My Dearest Emma,

By the 'Canopus', Captain Campbell, I have received all your truly kind and affectionate letters, from May 20th to July 3rd; with the exception of one, dated May 31st, sent to Naples.

This is the first communication I have had with England since we sailed.

All your letters, my dear letters, are so entertaining! and which paint so dearly what you are after, that they give either the greatest pleasure or pain. It is the next best thing to being with you.

I only desire, my dearest Emma, that you will always believe, that Nelson's your own; Nelson's Alpha and Omega is Emma! I cannot alter; my affection and love is beyond even this world! Nothing can shake it, but yourself; and that, I will not allow myself to think, for a moment, is possible.

I feel, that you are the real friend of my bosom, and dearer to me than life; and that I am the same to you. But I will neither have P's and Q's come near you! no; not the slice of Single Gloster! But if I was to go on, it would argue that want of confidence which would be injurious to your honour.

I rejoice that you have had so a pleasant a trip into Norfolk; and I hope, one day to carry you there by a nearer tie in law, but not in love and affection, than at present.

I wish you would never mention that person's name! It works up your anger, for no useful purpose. Her good or bad character, of me or thee, no one cares about. This letter will find you at dear Merton; where we shall one day meet, and be truly happy.

I do not think it can be a long war; and I believe, it will be much shorter than people expect; and I shall hope to find the new room built; the grounds laid out, neatly but not expensively; new Piccadilly gates; kitchen garden etc.; only let us have a plan, and then all will go on well. It will be a great source of amusement to you; and Horatia shall plant a tree. I dare say, she will be very busy.

Mrs Nelson, or Mrs Bolton, etc., will be with you; and time will pass away, till I have the inexpressible happiness of arriving at Merton. Even the thought of it vibrates through my nerves; for my love for you is as unbounded as the ocean!

I feel all your good mother's kindness; and, I trust we shall turn rich by being economists. Spending money, to please a pack of people, is folly, and without thanks. I desire, that you will say every kind thing from me to her, and make her a present of something in my name.

Dr Scott is gone with my mission to Algiers, or I would send you a copy of the King and Queen's letter. I send you one from the Queen. Both King, Queen and Acton, were very civil to Sir William Bolton. He dined with Acton.

Bolton does very well in his brig; but, he has made not a farthing of prize money. If I knew where to send him for some, he should go; but unless we have a Spanish War, I shall live here at great expence: although Mr Chevelier takes every care, and I have great reason to be satisfied.

I have just asked William, who behaves very well, whether he chooses to remit any of his wages to his father. It does not appear he does at present. He is paid by the King, eighteen pounds a year, as one of my retinue; therefore, I have nothing to pay. I have told him, whenever he chooses to send any, to tell Mr Scott, or Captain Hardy, and he will receive a remittance bill; so, he may now act as he pleases.

A-propos Mr Scott. He is very much obliged to you for your news of Mrs Scott's being brought to bed. No letters came in the cutter, but to me, and he was very uneasy. He is a very excellent good man; and, I am very fortunate in having such a one.

I admire your kindness to my dear sister Bolton. I have wrote her, that certainly I will assist Tom Bolton at college. It is better, as I tell her, not to promise more than I am sure I can perform. It is only doing them an injury.

I tell her, if vacancies, please God, should happen, that my income will be much increased.

With respect to Mr Bolton — everybody knows that I have no interest; nobody cares for me; but, if he will point out what he wants, I will try what can be done.

But, I am sure, he will not be half so well off as at present. Supposing he could get a place of a few hundreds a year, he would be a ten times poorer man than he is at present. I could convince you of it, in a moment; but, if I was to begin, then it would be said, I wanted inclination to render them a service.

I should like to see Sir H------P--------'s book. I cannot conceive how a man that is reported to have been so extravagant of government's money, to say no worse, can make a good story.

I wrote to the old Duke, not long since. I regard him; but I would not let him touch you for all his money. No; that would never do!

I believe Mr Bennett's bill to be correct; but it was not intended you should pay that out of the allowance for Merton; and how could you afford to send Mrs Bolton a hundred pounds. It is impossible, out of your income.

I wish Mr Addington would give you five hundred pounds a year; then you would be better able to give away than at present. But your purse, dear Emma, will always be empty; your heart is generous beyond your means.

Your good mother is always sure of my sincerest regard; pray, tell her so.

Conner is getting on very well; but I cannot ask Captain Capel to rate him; that must depend upon the boy's fitness, and Capel's kindness. I have placed another year's allowance of thirty pounds in Capel's hands, and given Conner a present.

What a story, about Oliver and Mr Matcham buying an estate in Holstein; and, to sell out at such a loss! I never heard the like. I sincerely hope it will answer his expectations; it is a fine country, but miserably cold.

How can Tyson be such a fool! I sincerely hope he will never want money. I am not surprised at Troubridge's abuse; but, his tongue is no scandal. You make me laugh when you imitate the Doctor!

I am quite delighted with Miss Yonge's goodness: and I beg you will make my best respects to her and her good father; and assure Mr Yonge, how much obliged I feel for all his kind attentions to you. Those who do that, are sure of a warm place in my esteem.

I have wrote to Dumourier; therefore I will only trouble you to say how much I respect him. I fancy he must have suffered great distress at Altona.

However, I hope, he will now be comfortable for life. He is a very clever man; and beats our generals, out and out. Don't they feel his coming? Advise him not to make enemies, by shewing he knows more than some of us. Envy knows no bounds to its persecution. He has seen the world, and will be on his guard.

I put Suckling into a frigate, with a very good man, who has become a schoolmaster; he does very well. Buckley will be a most excellent sea-officer; it is a pity he has not served his time. I have answered Mr Suckling's letter.

Gaetano is very well, and desires his duty. I think sometimes, that he wishes to be left at Naples; but I am not sure.

Mr Denis's relation has been long in the 'Victory'; but, if the Admiralty will not promote my lieutenants, they must all make a retrograde motion. But, I hope, they will not do such a cruel thing. I have had a very affectionate letter from Lord Minto. I hope George will be confirmed; but the Earl will not answer his application.

I shall send you some sherry, and a cask of paxoretti, by the convoy. Perhaps it had better go to Merton, at once; or, to Davison's cellar, where the wine-cooper can draw it off. I have two pipes of sherry, that is bad: but, if you like, you can send the Doctor a hogshead of that which is coming. Davison will pay all the duties. Send it entirely free, even to the carriage. You know, doing the thing well, is twice doing it; for sometimes carriage is more thought of than the prime cost.

The paxoretti I have given to Davison; and ordered one hogshead of sherry to Canterbury, and one to dear Merton.

My Dearest Emma,

What can I send you, buffeting the stormy gulph of Lyons; nothing, but my warmest affection, in return for all your goodness to me and mine!

I have sent to Naples, to try and get some shawls from the King's manufactory: and have requested Mr Falconer to ask his wife to choose some for you, and also some fine Venetian chains. I only wish, my dear Emma, that I knew what you would like, and I would order them with real pleasure; therefore, pray tell me.

We have so little communication with the Mediterranean world. Malta and Toulon are in separate worlds. It takes, on the average, six or seven weeks to get an answer to a letter; and in fifteen to twenty days, by the French papers, which we get from Paris, we have news from London; not the best side of the question, you may be sure, but enough to give us an idea of how matters go on.

I am of opinion that we shall have a peace much sooner than is generally expected; and that will be, to me, the very highest pleasure in this world; to return to Merton, and your dear beloved society.

Then, I agree with you, that "I would not give sixpence to call the King my uncle!"

I have wrote again to Gibbs about my Bronte affairs; and the copy of the a letter to Mrs Graefer I will send you, if I can; but you must preserve it, for I have no other. It may be necessary, situated as I am, to keep her in good humour; for a thousand pounds may be easily sold off the estate, and I never the wiser. However, you will see what I have said.

I have wrote to Me Elliot about Sabatello. What a rascal he must be! Gaetano is going to Naples, and I shall tell him; but, of course, he would rather favour Sabatello, his brother-in-law, than Julia.

I send you, my dearest Emma, one hundred pounds, which you will dispose of as follows — a present for yourself; and, if you like, a trifle for the servants; something to the poor of Merton; something for Mrs Cadogan, Miss Conner, Charlotte, etc., etc., I only send this as a trifling remembrance from me, whose whole soul is at Merton.

September 16th

The day after I wrote the former part of this letter Mr Scott received from Venice, and desired to present to you, two very handsome Venetian chains, received from Venice. This I would not suffer; for I allow no one to make my own Emma presents, but her Nelson. Therefore he will be paid for them; but your obligation is not the less to him. He is a very worthy, excellent, modest man, and an excellent secretary.

Dr Scott is, at times, wrong in the head; absolutely too much learning has turned him — but we all go on very well.

I had a letter from Gibbs about Bronte, and from Noble, which will begin another letter; only, believe me, at all times, sides, and ends, most faithfully yours, for ever,

Nelson & Bronte

September 26th, 1803

My Dearest Emma,

We have had, for these fourteen days past, nothing but gales of wind, and heavy sea. However, as our ships have suffered no damage, I hope to be able to keep the sea all the winter. Nothing, but dire necessity, shall force me to that out of the way place, Malta. If I had depended upon that island, for supplies for the fleet, we must all have been knocked up long ago; for Sir Richard Beckerton sailed from Malta, the same day I left Portsmouth, so we have been a pretty long cruise; and if I had only to look to Malta for supplies, our ships companies would have been done for long ago. However, by management I have got supplies from Spain, and also from France; but it appears, that we are almost shut out from Spain, for they begin to be very uncivil to our ships. However, I suppose, by this time, something is settled; but, I never hear from England. My last letters are July 6th, near three months. But as I get French newspapers occasionally, we guess how matters are going on.

I have wrote Mr Gibbs, again, a long history about Bronte; and, I hope, if General Acton will do nothing for me, that he will settle something; but, I know, whatever is settled, I shall be the loser.

Till next year, the debt will not be paid off; how----------------

"Victory" Off Toulon
October 18th, 1803

My Dearest Emma,

Your truly kind and affectionate letters, from July 17th to August 24th, all arrived safe in the Childers, the 6th of this month.

Believe me, my dearest Emma, that I am truly sensible of all your love and affection, which is reciprocal. You have, from the variety of incidents passing before you, much to tell me; and, besides, you have that happy knack of making everything you write interesting. Here I am, one day precisely like the other; except the difference of a gale of wind, or not.

Since September 1st, we have not had four fine days; and, if the French do not come out very soon, I fear some of my ships will cry out.

You are very good to send me your letters to read. Mrs D------- is a damned pimping bitch! What has she to do with your love? She would have pimped for Lord B-------, or Lord L--------, or Captain M'N--------, or anybody else.

She is all vanity; fancies herself beautiful; witty; in short, like you. She be damned!

As I wrote you, the consulship at Civita Vecchia will not, in itself, pay their lodgings; and, the bad air will tip her off.

There will be no Lord Bristol's table. He tore his last will, a few hours before his death. It is said, that it was giving every thing to those devils of Italians about him. I wish he may have given Mrs Dennis any thing; but I do not think it: and, as for you, my dear Emma, as long as I can, I don't want any of their gifts. As for old Q, he may put you into his will, or scratch you out, as he pleases. I care not.

If Mr Addington gives you a pension, it is well; but, do not let it fret you. Have you not Merton? It is clear — the first purchase — and my dear Horatia is provided for; and I hope, one of these days, that you will be my own Duchess of Bronte; and then, a fig for them all!

I have just had a letter from Gibbs, of which I send you a copy. You see what interest he is taking about Bronte.

I begin to think, without some assistance like his, that I should never have touched a farthing. It will be 1805 before I touch the estate. Neither principle or interest of the seven thousand ounces have been paid; and it is now eight thousand ounces debt.

You will see, Gibbs, at last, has fixed on sending his daughter home; And I shall be glad of so good an opportunity of obliging him, as it will naturally tie him to my interest. He was a great fool, not to have sent the child with you, as you wished.

I am glad to find, my dear Emma, that you mean to take Horatia home. Aye! she is like her mother; will have her own way, or kick up a devil of a dust. But you will cure her; I am afraid I should spoil her: for, I am sure, I would shoot any one who would hurt her.

She was always fond of my watch; and, very probably, I might have promised her one; indeed I gave her one, which cost sixpence! But I go nowhere to get anything pretty; therefore, do not think me neglectful.

I send you Noble's letter; therefore, I hope you will get your cases in good order: they have had some narrow escapes.

I am glad you liked Southend.

How that Coffin could come over, and palaver, Rowley, Keith, etc., and Coffin to abuse the Earl! Now, I can tell you, that he is the Earl's spy.

It is Coffin, who has injured Sir Andrew Hammond so much; and his custom is, to abuse the Earl, to get people to speak out; and then the Earl takes measures accordingly.

To me, it is nothing. Thank God! there can be no tales told of my cheating; Or, I hope, neglecting my duty. Whilst I serve, I will serve well, and closely; when I want a rest, I will go to Merton.

You know, my dear Emma, that I am never well when it blows hard. Therefore imagine what a cruise off Toulon is; even in summer time, we have a hard gale every week, and two days heavy swell.

It would kill you, and myself, to see you. Much less possible, to have Charlotte, Horatia, etc., on board ship!

And I, that have given orders to carry no women to sea in the "Victory", to be the first to break them!

And, as to Malta, I may never see it, unless we have an engagement; and, perhaps, not then; for, if it is complete, I may go home, for three months, to see you; but if you was at Malta, I might absolutely miss you, by leaving the Mediterranean without warning.

The other day we had a report the French were out, and seen steering to the westward. We were as far as Minorca, when the alarm was proved false.

Therefore, my dearest beloved Emma! although I should be the happiest of men, to live and die with you, yet my chance of seeing you is much more certain by your remaining at Merton, than wandering where I may never go; and certainly not to stay forty-eight hours.

You cannot, I am sure, more ardently long to see me, than I do to be with you; and if the war goes on, it is my intention to get leave to spend the next winter in England; but I verily believe that, long before that time, we shall have peace.

As for living in Italy, that is entirely out of the question. Nobody cares for us, there;

and, if I had Bronte — which thank God! I shall not — it would cost me a fortune to go there, and be tormented out of my life. I should never settle my affairs there.

I know, my own dear Emma, if she will let her reason have fair play, will say I am right; but she is, like Horatia, very angry, if she cannot have her own way. Here Nelson is called upon, in the most honourable manner, to defend his country! Absence, to us, is equally painful; but if I had either stayed at home, or neglected my duty abroad, would not my Emma have blushed for me?

She could never have heard of my praises, and how the country looks up.

I am writing, my dear Emma, to reason the point with you; and, I am sure you will see it in its true light. But I have said my say, on this subject, and will finish.

I have received your letter, with Lord William's and Mr Kemble's, about Mr Palmer: he is also recommended by the Duke of Clarence; and, he says, by desire of the Prince of Wales. I have, without him, twenty-six to be made Captains, and the list every day is increasing. It is not one whole French fleet that can get through it.

I shall, probably, offend many more than I can oblige. Such is always the case: like the tickets — those who get them, feel they have a right to them; and those who do not get them, feel offended for ever.

But, I cannot help it; I shall endeavour to do what is right, in every situation; and some ball may soon close all my accounts with this world of care and vexation!

But, never mind, my own dear beloved Emma; if you are true to me, I care not — and approve of all my actions. However, as you say, I approve of them myself; therefore probably, I am right.

Poor Reverend Scott is, I fear, in a very bad way. His head has been turned by too much learning, and the stroke of lightning will never let him be right again. The Secretary Scott is a treasure; and I am very well mounted: Hardy is everything I could wish or desire.

Our days pass so much alike that, having described one, you have them all. We now breakfast by candle-light; and all retire, at eight o'clock, to bed.

Naples, I fancy, is in a very bad way, in regard to money. They have not, or pretend not to have, enough to pay their officers; and I verily believe, if Acton was to give up his place, that it would become e province of France. Only think of Buonaparte's writing to the Queen, to desire her influence to turn out Acton! She answered, properly; at least, so says Mr Elliot, who knows more of Naples than any of us; God help him! — and General Acton has, I believe, more power than ever.

By Gibbs's letter, I see, he has sent over about my accounts at Bronte. He can have no interest in being unfriendly to me. Why should he be? I want no great matters from him; and he can want nothing from me, that it is not my duty to give his Sovereigns; therefore why should he be against us! For my part, my conduct will not alter, whether he is or not.

Our friend, Sir Alexander, is a very great diplomatic character; and, even an Admiral must not know what he is negotiating about: although you will scarcely believe, that the Bey of Tunis sent the man at my desire.

You shall judge — viz. 'The Tunisian Envoy is still here, negotiating. He is a moderate man; and, apparently, the best-disposed of any I ever did business with.' Could even the oldest diplomatic character be drier? I hate such parades of nonsense! But I will turn from such stuff.

You ask me, do you do right to give Charlotte things? I shall only say, my dear Emma, whatever you do in that way, I shall always approve. I only wish, I had more power than I have!

But somehow, my mind was not sharp enough for prize money — Lord Keith would have made twenty thousand pounds, and I have not made six thousand.

Poor Mr Este, how I pity him! but, what shall I do with him? However, if he comes, I shall shew him all the kindness in my power.

The vessel is just going off. I have not a scrap of news! Only, be assured of my most affectionate regards.

Remember me kindly to Charlotte. Shall always love those that are good to Horatia. I will write hereby another opportunity.

Remember me to Mrs Cadogan.

You may be sure, I do not forget Charles, who has not been well; Captain Capel is very good to him.

I am, ever, for ever, my dearest Emma, your most faithful and affectionate

Nelson & Bronte

My Own Dear Beloved Emma,

I received, on the 9th, your letters of September 29th, October 2, 7, 10, 12, 17th, November 5th, 8th, to the 24th; and I am truly sensible of all your kindness and affectionate regard for me; which, I am sure, is reciprocal, in every respect, from your own Nelson.

If that Lady Bitch knew of that person's coming to her house, it was a trick; but which, I hope, you will not subject yourself to again. But I do not like it!

However, it is passed; and we must have confidence in each other; and, my dearest Emma, judging of you by myself, it is not all the world that could seduce me, in thought, word, or deed, from all my sole holds most dear.

Indeed, if I can help it, I never intend to go out of the ship, but to the shore of Portsmouth; and that will be if it pleases God, before next Christmas. Indeed, I think, long before, if the French will venture to sea.

I send you a letter from the Queen of Naples. They call out, might and main, for our protection; and God knows, they are sure of me.

Mr Elliot complains heavily of the expence; and says he will retire the moment it is peace. He expected his family, when they would sit down eleven Elliots.

If, my dear Emma, you are to mind all the reports you may hear, you may always be angry with your Nelson.

In the first place, instead of eight days, Mr Acourt; he came on board one day, just before dinner, and left me next morning, after breakfast.

What pleasure people can have in telling lies! But, I care not what they say, I defy them all.

You may safely rely, that I can for ever repeat, with truth, these words — for ever I love you, and only you, my Emma; and, you may be assured, as long as you are the same to me, that you are never absent a moment from my thoughts.

I am glad you are going to Merton; you will live much more comfortable, and much cheaper, than in London; and this spring, if you like to have the house altered, you can do it. But, I fancy, you will soon tire of so much dirt, and the inconvenience will be very great the whole summer.

All I request, if you fix to have it done, is that Mr Davison's architect, who drew the plan, may have the inspection; and he must take care that it does not exceed the estimate.

If it is done by contract, you must not alter; or a bill is run up, much worse than if we never contracted. Therefore, I must either buy the materials, and employ respectable workmen, under the architect, or contract.

I rather believe, it would be better for me to buy the materials, and put out the building to a workman; but you must get some good advice.

With respect to the new entrance .................

Young Faddy, my Dearest Emma, brought me, two days ago, your dear and most kind letter of November 26th, and you are sure that I shall take a very early opportunity of promoting him; and he appears to be grown a fine young man, but vacancies do not happen very frequently in this station. However, if he behaves well, he may be sure of me.

With respect to Mr Jefferson, I can neither say nor do anything. The surgeon of the 'Victory' is a very able, excellent man, and the ship is kept in the most perfect state of health; and, I would not, if I could — but, thank God, I cannot — do such an unjust act, as to remove him. He is my own asking for! and I have every reason to be perfectly content.

Mr Jefferson got on, by my help: and, by his own misconduct he got out of a good employ, and has seen another person, at Malta hospital, put over his head. He must now begin again; and act with much more attention and sobriety, than he has done, to ever get forward again; but, time may do much: and, I shall rejoice to hear of his reformation.

I am not surprised, my dearest Emma, at the enormous expences of the watering-place; but, if it has done my own Emma service, it is well laid out. A thousand pounds a year will not go far; and we need to be great economists, to make both ends meet, and to carry on the little improvements. As for making one farthing more prize money, I do not expect it:

except for taking the French fleet; and the event of that day, who can foresee!

With respect to Mrs Graefer — what she has done, God and herself knows; but I have made up my mind, that Gibbs will propose a hundred pounds a year for her; if so I shall grant it and have done. I send you Mrs Graefer's last letter.

Whilst I am on the subject of Bronte, I have one more word — and your good, kind heart, must not think that I shall die one hour the sooner; on the contrary, my mind has been more content ever since I have done; I have left you a part of the rental of Bronte, to be paid every half year, and in advance. It is but common justice; and, whether Mr Addington gives you anything, or not, you will want it.

I would not have you lay out more than is necessary at Merton. The rooms, and the new entrance, will take a great deal of money. The entrance by the corner, I would have certainly done; a common white gate will do for the present, and one of the cottages, which is in the barn, can be put up, as a temporary lodge. The road can be made to a temporary bridge; for that part of the Nile, one day, shall be filled up.

Downing's canvas awning will do for a passage. For the winter, the carriage can be put in the barn; and, giving up Mr Bennett's premises, will save fifty pounds a year; and, another year, we can fit up the coach- house and stables which are in the barn.

The footpath should be turned. I did show Mr Haslewood the way I wished it done; and Mr…….. will have no objections, if we make it better than ever it has been; and I also beg, as my dear Horatia is to be at Merton, that a strong netting, about three feet high, may be placed around the Nile, that the little thing may not tumble in; and then, you may have ducks again in it. I forget, at what place we saw the netting; and either Mr Perry, or Mr Goldsmith told us where it was to be bought. I shall be very anxious until I know this is done.

I have had no very late opportunities of sending to Naples; but via Malta, I wrote to Gibbs, to desire he would send over and purchase the amorins. They will arrive in time. I hope, the watch is arrived safe.

The 'British Fair' cutter, I hope, is arrived safe. She has three packets, from me, to England.

The expences of the alterations to Merton you are not to pay from the income. Let it all be put to a separate account, and I will provide a fund for the payment.

All I long for, just now, is to hear that you perfectly recovered; and, then, I care for nothing; all my hopes are, to see you, and be happy, at dear Merton, again, but, I fear, this miscarriage of Pichegru's in France, will prolong the war. It has kept the French fleet in port, which we are all sorry for.

Sir William Bolton was on board yesterday. He looks thin. The fag in a brig is very great; and I see no prospect of his either making prize money, or being made post, at present; but, I shall omit no opportunity.

I wrote Mrs Bolton a few months ago; and gave her letter yesterday, to Bolton. He conducts himself very well indeed.

Ever, my dearest Emma, for ever, I am your most faithful and affectionat

## Nelson & Bronte

Although I cannot well afford it, yet I could not bear that poor blind Mrs Nelson should be in want in her old days, and sell her plate; therefore, if you will find out what are her debts, If they come within my power, I will certainly pay them.

Many, I dare say, if they had commanded here, would have made money; but, I can assure you, for prizes taken in the Mediterranean, I have not more than paid my expences. However, I would rather pinch myself, than she, poor soul, should want. Your good angelic heart, my dearest beloved Emma, will truly agree with me, everything is very expensive; and, even if we find it, and will be obliged to economise, if we assist our friends: and, I am sure, we should find more comfort in it than loaded tables, and entertaining a set of people who care not for us.

An account is this moment brought me, that a small sum is payable to me, for some neutral taken off Cadiz in May 1800; so that I shall not be poorer for my gift. It is odd, is it not?

I shall, when I come home, settle four thousand pounds in trustee's hands, for Horatia; for, I will not put it in my power to have her left destitute: for she would want friends, if we left her in this world. She shall be independent of any smiles or frowns!

I am glad you are going to take her home; and if you will take the trouble with Eliza and Ann, I am the very last to object.

Tom, I shall certainly assist at college; and, I am sure, the Doctor expects that I should do the same for Horace: but I must make my arrangements, so as not to run in debt.

April 9th.

I have wrote to the Duke; but, by your account, I fear he is not alive. I write because you wish me; and because, I like the Duke, and hope he will leave you some money. But, for myself, I can have no right to expect a farthing: nor would I be a legacy hunter for the world; I never knew any good come from it.

I send you a letter from Mr Falconet. I am afraid, they have made a jumble about the amorins. And I send you a very impertinent letter from that old cat. I have sent her a very dry answer; and told her, I should send the sweetmeats to you. I always hated the old bitch! But, was she young, and as beautiful as an angel, I am engaged; I am all, soul and body, my Emma's; nor would I would I change her for all this world could give me.

I would not have Horatia think of a dog. I shall not bring her one; and, I am sure, she is better without a pet of that sort. But, she is like her mother, would get all the dogs in the place about her.

April 14th

I am so sea sick, that I cannot write another line; except, to say, –God Almighty bless you, my dearest Emma! prays, ever, your faithful

Nelson & Bronte

I have, my Dearest Beloved Emma, been so uneasy for this last month; desiring, most ardently, to hear of your well doing!

Captain Capel brought me your letters sent by the 'Thisbe', from Gibraltar. I opened — opened — found none but December, and early January. I was in such agitation! At last, I found one, without a date, which, thank God, told my poor heart, that you was recovering, but that dear little Emma was no more! and that Horatia had been so ill — it all together upset me.

But it was just at bed-time; and I had time to reflect, and be thankful to God for sparing you and our dear Horatia. I am sure, the loss of one — much more, both — would have drove me mad. I was so agitated, as it was, that I was glad it was night, and that I could be by myself.

Kiss dear Horatia for me; tell Mrs G. that I shall certainly settle a small pension on her. It shall not be large, as we may have the pleasure of making her little presents; and, my dearest Emma, I shall not be wanting to everybody, who has been kind to you, be they servants or gentle folks.

Admiral Lutwidge is a good man; and I like Mrs Lutwidge — and shall, always more, because she is fond of you.

Never mind the great Bashaw at the Priory. He be damned! If he was single, and had a mind to marry you, he could only make you a Marchioness; but as he is situated, and I situated, I can make you a Duchess; and if it pleases God, that time may arrive! Amen, Amen.

As for your friend Lady H......., she is, in her way, as great a pimp as any of them. What a set! But if they manage their own intrigues, is not that enough! I am sure, neither you or I care what they do! much less, envy them their 'chere amies'.

As for Lord S.........., and the other, I care nothing about them; for I have every reason, by my own feelings towards you, to think you care only for your Nelson.

I have not heard of your receiving the little box from Naples, bracelets, I fancy, But I did not open them.

I wish the amorins may come in time for the conveyance to Captain Layman, who has, most unfortunately, lost his sloop: he is strongly recommended, by the governor and garrison of Gibraltar. But perhaps, he may not be able to obtain it.

We have such reports about the King's health, that the present ministry may be out; and for what I know or care, another set may be no better, for you or me.

As for the Admiralty, let who will be in, they can neither do me any great good or harm; they may vex me, a little; but, that will recoil upon themselves.

I hope, however, they will conform Captain Layman; for he is attached not only to me, but is a very active officer. But, it was his venturing to know more about India than Troubridge, that made them look shy upon him; and, his tongue runs too fast. I often tell him, not to let his tongue run so fast, or his pen write so much.

*Nelson & Bronte*

My Dearest Emma,

I have received all you your truly kind and affectionate letters, to January 25th, by the 'Thisbe'; and, last night, your letter of January 13th, by Naples.

The amorins will go under the care of Captain Layman; who, unfortunately, lost his sloop, but, with much credit to himself, he has been acquitted of all blame.

I rejoice that dear Horatia is got well: and also, that you, my dearest Emma, are recovered of your severe indisposition. In our present situation with Spain, this letter, probably, may never reach you.

I have wrote fully, and intend to send them by the 'Argus', who I expect to join every minute.

Elphi Bey, I hear, has had all his fine things taken from him. He escaped into the Desert, and is pursued; probably, his head is off, long before this time.

The French fleet came out on the 5th, but went in again the next morning. Yesterday, a Rear-Admiral, and seven sail of ships, including frigates, put their noses outside the harbour. If they go on playing this game, some day we shall lay salt upon their tails; and so end the campaign of, my dearest Emma, your most faithful and affectionate,

## Nelson & Bronte

I am glad to hear that you are going to take my dear Horatia, to educate her. She must turn out an angel, if she minds what you say to her; and Eliza and Ann will never forget your goodness.

My health is so, so! I shall get through the summer; and in the winter shall go home. You will readily fancy all I would say and do think.

My kind love to all friends.

My Dearest Emma,

I had wrote you a line, intended for the 'Swift' cutter; but instead of her joining me, I had the mortification, not only to hear that she was taken, but that all the dispatches and letters had fallen into the hands of the enemy: a very pretty piece of work!

I am not surprised at the capture; but am very much so that any dispatches should be sent in a vessel with twenty-three men, not able to cope with any row-boat privateer. As I do not know what letters of your's are in her, I cannot guess what will be said. I suppose there will be a publication.

The loss of the 'Hindostan', was great enough; but for importance, it is lost, in comparison to the probable knowledge the enemy will obtain of our connections with foreign countries. Foreigners for ever say — and it is true — "We dare not trust England; one way, or other, we are sure to be committed!" However, it is now too late to launch out on this subject.

Not a thing has been saved out of the 'Hindostan', not a second shirt for any one; and it has been by extraordinary exertions, that the people's lives were saved.

Captain Hallowell is so good to take home, for me, wine as by the enclosed list; and, if I can, some honey. The Spanish honey is so precious, that if any one has a cut, or sore throat, it is sure to cure it.

I mention this, in case you should wish to give the Duke a jar. The smell is wonderful! It is to be produced no where, but in the mountains near Rosas. The Cyprus wine, one hogshead was for Buonaparte.

I would recommend the wine-cooper drawing it off: and you can send a few dozens to the Duke: who I know, takes a glass every day at two o'clock.

I wish I had anything else to send you; but, my dearest Emma, you must take the will for the deed.

I am pleased with Charlotte's letter and, as she loves my dear Horatia, I shall always like her. What hearts those must have who do not! But thank God, she shall not be dependent on any of them.

Your letter of February 12th through Mr Falconet, I have received.

I know they are all read; therefore, never sign your name. I shall continue to write, through Spain; but never say a word that can convey any information — except, of eternal attachment and affection for you, and that, I care not, who knows: for I am, for ever, and ever, your only your

Nelson & Bronte

Poor Captain Le Gros had your note to him in his pocket-book, and that was all he saved. Mr Este left him at Gibraltar and went to Malta in the 'Thisbe'

Captain Le Gros is now trying. I think, it will turn out that every person is obliged to his conduct for saving their lives.

She took fire thirteen leagues from the land.

"Victory" April 23rd, 1804

My Dearest Emma,

Hallowell has promised me, if the Admiralty will give him leave to go to London, that he will call at Merton.

His spirit is certainly more independent than almost any man's I ever knew, but, I believe he is attached to me. I am sure, he has no reason to be so, to either Troubridge or anyone at the Admiralty.

I have sent, last night, a box of Marischino Veritabile of Zara, which I got Jemmy Anderson to buy for me, and twelve bottles of Tokay. I had better keep none for myself, being better pleased that you should have it.

I am, ever, and for ever, your most faithful and affectionate

Nelson & Bronte

Hallowell parted last night; but being in sight, I am sending a frigate with a letter to the Admiralty.

May God almighty bless you, and send us a happy meeting!

85

I did not, my dearest Emma, pass over the 26th without thinking of you in the most affectionate manner, which the truest love and affectionate regard of man to a dear beloved woman, which could enter into my mind.

I have been for some days, and am still, very unwell, without being seriously ill, but I fret absolutely like a fool for the faults of others. It was no fault of mine that the dispatches were taken, but of those who sent them in a vessel not fit to trust my old shoes in; nor is it my fault that the 'Kent', the finest ship in the fleet, is kept so long from England, notwithstanding my representations that she is now obliged to leave the fleet, to lay guard-ship at Naples, and more will very soon be in as bad a plight. My only wish is for the coming out of the French fleet to finish all my uneasinesses. But I yet trust that the reign of Buonaparte will soon be over, and then that we shall have a few years of peace and quietness.

Remember me kindly to all we hold most dear, and be assured, my dear Emma, that I am for ever and ever, and if possible more than ever, yours most faithfully, &c.,

Captain Layman, Captain Hallowell, and I believe another packet of letters for you, are now at Gibraltar.

I find, my Dearest Emma, that your picture is very much admired by the French Consul at Barcelona; and that he has not sent it to be admired — which, I am sure, it would be — by Buonaparte.

They pretend, that there were three pictures taken. I wish, I had them: but they are all gone, as irretrievably as the dispatches; unless we may read them in a book, as we printed their correspondence from Egypt.

But, from us, what can they find out! That I love you, most dearly: and hate the French, most damnably.

Dr Scott went to Barcelona, to try to get the private letters: but I fancy, they are all gone to Paris. The Swedish and American Consuls told him, that the French Consul had your picture, and read your letters; and Doctor thinks, one of them probably read the letters.

By the master's account of the cutter, I would not have trusted a pair of old shoes in her. He tells me she did not sail, but was a good sea boat.

I hope Mr Marsden will not trust any more of my private letters in such a conveyance; if they choose to trust the affairs of the public in such a thing, I cannot help it.

I long for the invasion to be over; it must finish the war, and I have no fear for the event.

I do not say, all I wish; and which my dearest beloved Emma (- read that, whoever opens this letter; and, for what I care, publish it to the world) - your fertile imagination can readily fancy I would say: but this I can say, with great truth, that I am for ever yours

--------------

My Dearest Emma,

Yesterday, I took Charles Conner on board, from the 'Phoebe', to try what we can do with him. At present, poor fellow, he has got a very bad eye — and, I almost fear that he will be blind of it — owing to an olive stone striking his eye: but the surgeon of the "Victory", who is by far the most able medical man I have ever seen, and equally so as a surgeon, says that, if it can be saved, he will do it.

The other complaint, in his head, is but little more, I think than it was when he first came to Deal: a kind of silly laugh, when spoken to. He always complains of a pain in the back part of his head; but when that is gone, I do not perceive but that he is as wise as many of his neighbours.

You may rely, my dear Emma, that nothing shall be wanting, on my part, to render him every service.

Capel — although, I am sure, very kind to younkers — I do not think, has the knack of keeping them in high discipline, he lets them be their own master too much.

I paid Charlie's account, yesterday; since he has been in the 'Phoebe', one hundred and fifty-five pounds, fourteen shillings. However, he must now turn over a new leaf; and I sincerely hope, poor fellow, he will yet do well.

I wrote you on the 22nd through Rosas, in Spain, and I shall write, in a few days, by Barcelona: this goes by Gibraltar.

I have wrote Admiral Lutwidge: Mrs Lutwidge must wait, for I cannot get through all my numerous letters: for, whoever writes, although upon their own affairs, are offended if they are not answered.

I have not seen young Bailey; I suppose, he is in the 'Leviathan'.

By the parcel, I see he is in the 'Canopus' and I can, at present, be of no use to him.

May 30th.

Charles is very much recovered.

I write you, this day, by Barcelona. Your dear phiz — but not the least like you — on the cup, is safe: but I would not use it, for the world; for, if it was broke, it would distress me very much.

Your letters, by the 'Swift', I shall never get back. The French Consul, at Barcelona, is bragging that he has three pictures of you from the 'Swift'. I do not believe him: but what if he had a hundred! Your resemblance is so deeply engraved in my heart, that there it can never be effaced; and who knows? some day, I may have the happiness of having a living picture of you!

Old mother L......... is a damned b......; but I do not understand what you mean, or what plan.

I am not surprised at my friend Kingsmill admiring you, and forgetting Mary: he loves variety, and handsome women.

You touch upon the old Duke; but I am dull of comprehension; believing you all my own. I cannot imagine any one else to offer, in any way. We have enough, with prudence; and, without it, we should soon be beggars, if we had five times as much.

I see, Lord Stafford is going to oppose Mr Addington; the present ministry cannot stand. I wish Mr Addington had given you the pension; Pitt, and hard-hearted Grenville, never will.

What a fortune the death of Lord Camelford gives him!

Everything you tell me about my dear Horatia charms me. I think I see her, hear her, and admire her: but she is like her dear, dear mother.

I am sorry if your account of George Martin's wife is correct: he deserves a better fate. But he is like Foley; give up a great deal, to marry the relation of a great man: although, in fact, she is no relation to the Duke of Portland.

I wish, I could but be at dear Merton, to assist in making the alterations. I think I should have persuaded you to have kept the pike, and a clear stream; and to have put all the carp, tench, and fish who muddy the water into the pond. But, as you like, I am content. Only take care, that my darling does not fall in, and get drowned. I begged you to get the little netting along the edge, and, particularly, on the bridges.

I admire the seal; and God bless you, also! Amen.

The boy, South, is on board another ship learning how to be a musician. He will return soon, when he shall have the letter and money. I hope, he will deserve it, but he has been a very bad boy; but good floggings, I hope, will save him from the gallows.

Mr Fallows is a clever man. He would not have made such a blunder as our friend Drake, and Spencer Smith. I hear, the last is coming, via Trieste, to Malta. Perhaps he wants to get to Constantinople; and, if the Spencers get in, the Smiths will get any thing.

Mr Elliot, I hear, is a candidate for it. He complains of the expence of Naples, I hear; and, that he cannot make both ends meet, although he sees no company.

The histories of the Queen are beyond whatever I have heard from Sir William. Prince

Leopold's establishment is all French. The Queen's favourite, Lieutenant-Colonel St Clair, is a subaltern; Latour, the Captain in the navy; and, another!

However, I never touch on these matters; for, I care not how she amuses herself. It will be the upset of Acton; or rather, he will not, I am told, stay. The King is angry with her; his love is long gone by.

I have only one word more — Do not believe a syllable the newspapers say, or what you hear. Mankind seems fond of telling lies.

Remember me kindly to Mrs Cadogan, and all our mutual friends; and be assured, I am, for ever, my dearest Emma, you most faithful and affectionate

*Nelson & Bronte*

George Campbell desires me always to present his best respects; and make mine, to good Mr Yonge. What can I write him? I am sure, he must have great pleasure in attending you: and, when you see Sir William Scott, make my best regards acceptable to him. There is no man I have a higher opinion of, both as a public and private character.

You will long ago have had my letter; with one to Davison, desiring he will pay for the alterations to Merton. I shall send you a letter for the hundred pounds a month, to the Bank.

Since I wrote you, my dearest Emma, on the 30th and 31st May, nothing now has happened; except our hearing the 'feu de joie' at Toulon, for the declaration of the Emperor.

What a capricious nation those French must be! However, I think, it must in any way, be advantageous to England. There ends, for a century, all republics.

By vessels from Marseilles, the French think it will be a peace; and they say that several of their merchant ships are fitting out. I earnestly pray, that it may be so; and, that we may have a few years of rest.

I rather believe, my antagonist at Toulon, begins to be angry with me: at least, I am trying to make him so; and then he may come out, and beat me, as he says he did, off Boulogne.

He is the Admiral that went to Naples in December 1792, La Touche Treville, who landed the grenadiers. I owe him something for that.

I am better, my dear Emma, than I have been, and shall get through the summer very well; and I have the pleasure to tell you, that Charles is very much recovered. There is no more the matter with his intellects, than with mine! Quite the contrary; he is very quick.

Mr Scott, who has overlooked all his things, says, his clothes, etc., are in the highest order he has ever seen. I shall place him in the 'Niger', with Captain Hilliar, when he joins; but, all our ships are so full, that it is very difficult to get a birth for one in any ship.

Would you conceive it possible! but it is now from April 2nd, since I have heard direct from Ball. The average time for a frigate to go, and return, is from six to seven weeks. From you, I had letters, April 5th, and the papers to April 8th, received May 10th with a convoy.

This goes through friend Gaynor.

Sir William Bolton joined last night; and received his letters, announcing his being called papa. He is got a very fine young man and good officer. Lord St Vincent has desired he may have the first Admiralty vacancy; but nobody will die, or go home.

A-propos! I believe you should buy a piece of plate, value fifty pounds, for our god-daughter of Lady Bolton; and something of twenty or thirty pounds value, for Colonel Suckling's.

But, my Emma, you are not to pay for them, let it rest for me; or if the amount is sent me, I will order payment.

Remember me most kindly to Horatia, good Mrs Cadogan, Charlotte, Miss Connor, and all our friends at dear, dear Merton: where, from my soul, I wish I was, this moment: then, I sincerely hope, we should have no cause for sorrow.

You will say what is right to Mr Perry, Newton, Patterson, Mr Lancaster, etc., you know all these matters. God in heaven bless and preserve you, for ever! prays, ever, yours most faithfully,

My Dearest Emma,

I wrote to you, on the 6th, via the 'Rosa': this goes by Barcelona; to which place I am sending Sir William Bolton, to fetch Dr Scott, who is gone there, poor fellow, for the benefit of his health!

I have just had very melancholy letters from the King and Queen of Naples on account of General Acton's going to Sicily. The insolence of Buonaparte was not to be parried without a war; for which they are unable, if unassisted.

I have letters from Acton, May 28, on board the 'Archimedes', just going into Palermo. He will probably return to Naples, unless new events arise; and that may be; for a minister, once out, may find some difficulty in renewing his post. He has acted with great and becoming spirit.

I am better, but I have been very unwell. It blows here, as much as ever. Yesterday was a little hurricane of a wind.

I daresay, Prince Castelcicala knows it by express; if not, you may tell him, with my best respects.

He, and everyone else, may be sure of my attachment to those good Sovereigns. By this route, I do not choose to say more on this subject.

With my kindest regards to Horatia and your good mother, Charlotte, Miss C, and all our friends, believe me, my dear Emma, for ever, your most faithful and affectionate,

---------

I fear Sardinia will be invaded from Corsica before you get this letter. I have not small ships to send there, or anywhere else; not in the proportion of one to five.

You may communicate this to Mr Addington, if you think he does not know it; but, to no one else, except Castelcicala; of which relates to Naples.

I have very flattering letters from the Grand Vizier, in the name of the Sultan: and from Cadir, now Captain Pacha.

Although I have wrote you, my dearest Emma, a letter, by Rosas, of 27th June, not yet gone, the weather being so very bad, that ships cannot get across the gulf of Lyons, yet I will not miss the opportunity of writing by Gibraltar.

You must not, my Emma, think of hearing from me by way of Malta: it takes as long to send a letter to Malta, as to England.

The 'Monmouth,' which you complain of not hearing by, I knew nothing if her movements for some months before. The ships from Malta with the convoys, pick up our letters at Gibraltar. Therefore, do not hurt my feelings, by telling me that I neglect any opportunity of writing.

Your letters of April 13th, 22nd and May 13th, through Mr Falconet, came safe, a few days ago. Mr Falconet is the French banker; and he dare not buy a little macaroni for me, or let an Englishman into his house.

Gibbs is still at Palermo; I fancy, he will make a good thing of my estate; however, I wish it was settled. He wrote me, a short time since, that he wished I would give him a hint (but without noticing that it came from him) that I thought Mrs Graefer and her child had better go to England; on pretence of educating her daughter, etc. But I would have nothing to do with any such recommendation. It would end in her coming to me, in England; and saying, that she could not live upon what she had, and that I advised her to come to England, or she should not have thought of it.

In short, Gibbs wants to remove her. He is afraid of his pocket, I fancy; and the daughter is, I fancy, now in some seminary at Palermo, at Gibbs's expence. I wrote him word, fully, I would advise no such thing; she was to form her own judgement.

What our friends are after at Naples, they best know. The poor King is miserable at the loss of Acton. The Queen writes to me about honest Acton, etc., etc., and I hear, that she has been the cause of ousting him: and they say - her enemies — that her conduct is all French. That, I do not believe, although she is likely to be the dupe of French 'emigres' who always beset her.

I doubt much, my dear Emma, even her constancy of real friendship to you; although, in my letter on Acton, which Mr Elliot says he read to her, I mentioned the obligations she was under, to you, etc., etc., in very strong terms.

What could the name of the minister signify! It was the letter which was wanted to the Prime Minister.

But, never mind; with prudence, we shall do very well.

I have wrote to Davison, by land, who, I am very sorry for: but, he never would take a friend's caution, and he had been severely bit.

Your accounts of Merton delight me; and you will long ago have known, that I have directed the bills for the alterations to be paid my expences these last nine months.

I shall expect to eat my Christmas dinner at Merton; unless those events happen which I can neither foresee nor prevent.

I am not well; and must have rest, for a few months, even should the want me; which, very likely, they will not. News, I can have none.

April 9th, ' Leviathan' sailed; so government don't care much for us.

Kiss my dear Horatia, for me! I hope you will have her at Merton; and, believe me, my dear Emma, that I am, for ever, as ever, your attached, faithful and affectionate

Nelson & Bronte

Although, my Dearest Emma, from the length of time my other letters have been getting to you, I cannot expect that this will share a better fate; yet as the 'Childers' is going to Rosas, to get us some news from Paris - which is the only way I know of what is passing in England - I take my chance of the post; but I expect the 'Kent' will be in England d before this letter; and by which ship I write to the Admiralty relative to my health.

Therefore, I shall only say, that I hope a little of your good nursing, with ass's milk will set me up for another campaign; should the Admiralty wish me to return, in the spring, for another year; but I own, I think we shall have peace.

The 'Ambuscade' arrived this day fortnight, with our victuallers, etc., and very acceptable they were. By her, I received your letters of May 14th, 22nd, and 30th, via Lisbon; and, of April 9th, 18th, 15th, May 10th, 18th, 29th, June 1st, 5th through, I suppose, the Admiralty.

The box you mention, is not arrived; nor have I a scrap of a pen from Davidson. The weather in the Mediterranean seems much altered. In July seventeen days the fleet was in a gale of wind.

I have often wrote to Davison, to pay for all the improvements at Merton. The new building the chamber over the dining room you must consider. The stair window, we settled, was not to be stopped up. The underground passage will, I hope be made; but I shall, please God, soon see it all. I have wrote you, my dear Emma, about Horatia; but by the 'Kent' I shall write fully. May God bless you, my dearest best-beloved Emma! and believe me, ever, your most faithful and affectionate, ---------

Kind love, and regards, to Mrs Cadogan, and all friends, God bless you, again and again.

My Dearest Emma,

The 'Kent' left us three days ago; and, as the wind has been perfectly fair since her departure, I think she will have a very quick passage, and arrive long before this letter. But, as a ship is going to Rosas, I will not omit the opportunity of writing through Spain; as you say, the letters all arrive safe.

We have nothing but gales of wind; and I have had for two days, fires in the cabin, to keep out the very damp air. I still hope that, by the time of my arrival in England, we shall have peace. God send it!

I have not yet received your muff; I think probably I shall bring it with me.

I hope Davison has done the needful in paying for the alterations at Merton. If not, it is not too late; and we will fix a complete plan, and execute it next summer. I shall be clear of debt, and what I have will be my own.

God bless you! Amen. Amen.

George Elliot goes to Malta, for a convoy to England, this day.

If you ever see Lord Minto, say so.

-----------

*My Ever Dearest Emma,*

Yesterday, I wrote to you, through Spain; this goes by Naples. Mr Falconet, I think, will send it, although I am sure, he feels great fear from the French ministry, for having anything to do with us.

Mr Greville is a shabby fellow! It never could have been the intention of Sir William, but that you should have had seven hundred pounds a year neat money; for when he made the will, the Income Tax was double what it is at present; and the estate what it is paid from is increasing every year in value.

It may be law but it is not just; nor in equity would, I believe, be considered as the will and intention of Sir William. Never mind! Thank God, you do not want any of his kindness; nor will he give you justice. I may say all this; because my actions are different, even to a person who has treated me so ill.

As to ------, I know the full extent of the obligation I owe him, and he may be useful to me again; but I can never forget his unkindness to you. But, I guess, many reasons influenced his conduct, in bragging of his riches, and my honourable poverty; but, as I have said, and with honest pride, what I have is my own; it never cost the widow a tear, or the nation a farthing. I got what I have with my pure blood, from the enemies of my country. Our house, my dear Emma, is built upon a solid foundation; and will last to us, when his house and lands may belong to others than his children.

I would not have believed it, from anyone but you! But, if ever I go abroad again, matters shall be settled very differently.

I am working hard with Gibbs about Bronte, but the calls upon me are very heavy. Next September, I shall be clear; I mean September 1805.

I have wrote both to Acton and the Queen about you. I do not think she likes Mr Elliot; and therefore, I wish she had never shown him my letters about you. We also know, that he has a card of his own to play.

Dr Scott, who is a good man — although, poor fellow! very often wrong in the head — is going with Staines, in the 'Cameleon', just to take a peep at Naples and Palermo. Have introduced him to Acton, who is very civil to everybody from me.

The Admiralty proceedings towards you, you will know much sooner than I shall. I hope they will do the thing handsomely, and allow of my return in the spring but, I do not expect it.

I am very uneasy at your and Horatia being on the coast; for you cannot move, if the French make the attempt; which, I am told, they have done and been repulsed. Pray God, it may be true!

I shall rejoice to hear you and Horatia are safe at Merton; and happy shall I be, the day I join you. Gannam Justem.

Gaetano is very grateful for your remembrance of him. Mr Chevalier is an excellent servant. William says, he has wrote twice; I suppose he thinks that enough.

This is written within three miles of the fleet in Toulon, who are looking very tempting. Kind regards to Mrs Cadogan, Charlotte, etc., and compliments to all our joint friends; for they are no friends of mine, who are not friends to Emma. God bless you, again and again!

Captain Hardy has not been very well; and, I fancy, Admiral Murray will not be sorry to see England; especially since he has been promoted......... he expects his flag may get up.

God bless you, my dearest Emma; and, be assured, I am ever most faithfully yours.

This day, my dearest Emma, which gave me birth, I consider as more fortunate than common days; as by my coming into this world, it has brought me so intimately acquainted with you, who my soul holds most dear. I well know that you will keep it, and have my dear Horatia to drink my health.

Forty six years of toil and trouble! How few more, the common lot of mankind leads us to expect; and, therefore, it is almost time to think of spending the few last years in peace and quietness!

By this time, I should think, either my successor is named, or permission is granted me to come home; and, if so, you will not long receive this letter before I make my appearance: which will make us, I am sure, both truly happy.

We have had nothing, for this fortnight, but gales of easterly winds, and heavy rains; not a vessel of any kind, or sort, joined the fleet.

I was in hopes Dr Scott would have returned from Naples, and that I could have told you something comfortable for you from that quarter: and it is now seven weeks since we heard from Malta. Therefore, I know nothing of what is passing in the world.

I would not have you, my dear Emma, allow the work of brick and mortar to go on in the winter months. It can all be finished next summer; when I hope, we shall have peace, or such an universal war as will upset that vagabond Buonaparte.

I have been tolerable well, till this last bad weather, which has given me pains in my breast; but, never mind, all will be well when I get to Merton.

Admiral Campbell, who is on board, desires to be remembered to you. He does not like much to stay here, after my departure. Indeed, we all draw so well together in the fleet, that I flatter myself the sorrow of my departure will be pretty general.

Admiral Murray will be glad to get home; Hardy is as good as ever; and Mr Secretary Scott is an excellent man. God bless you, my dearest Emma! and, be assured I am ever your most faithful and affectionate.

*Nelson & Bronte*

Kiss dear Horatia. I hope she is at Merton <u>fixed</u>

I wrote you, my dearest Emma, this morning, by way of Lisbon; but a boat, which is going to Torbay, having brought out a cargo of potatoes, will I think get home before the Lisbon packet.

I shall only say — Guzelle Gannam Justem — and that I love you beyond all the world!

This may be read by French, Dutch, Spanish or Englishmen; for, it comes from the heart of, my Emma, your faithful and affectionate

## Nelson Bronte

I think the gentry will soon come out. I cannot say more by such a conveyance.

My Dearest Emma,

The dreadful effects of the yellow fever, at Gibraltar, and many parts of Spain, will naturally give you much uneasiness; till you hear that, thank God, we are entirely free from it, and in the most perfect health, not one man being ill in the fleet. The cold weather will, I hope, cure the disorder.

Whilst I am writing this letter, a cutter is arrived from England with strong indications of a Spanish war.

I hope from my heart, that it will not prove one. But however that is, my die is cast; and, long before this time, I expect another Admiral is far on his way to supersede me. Lord Keith, I think a very likely man.

I should, for your sake, and for many of our friends, have liked an odd hundred thousand pounds; but never mind. If they give me the choice of staying a few months longer, it will be very handsome; and, for the sake of others, we would give up, my dear Emma, very much of our own felicity. If they do not, we shall be happy with each other, and with dear Horatia.

The cutter returns with my answers directly; therefore, my own dear Emma, you must only fancy all my thoughts and feelings towards you. They are everything which a fond heart can fancy.

I have not a moment; I am writing and signing orders, whilst I am writing to my own Emma.

My life, my soul, God in Heaven bless you!

Your letter is September 16th, your last is August 27th. I have not made myself understood about Mrs Bolton's money. You give away too much.

Kiss our dear Horatia a thousand times, for your own faithful Nelson. I send two hundred pounds, keep it for your own pocket money.

You must tell Davison, and Haslewood, that I cannot answer their letters. Linton cannot be fixed; but you will know whether I come home, or stay, from Mr Marsden.

God bless you!

Tell my brother, that I have made Mr Yonge a Lieutenant, into the 'Seahorse' frigate, Captain Boyle.

Once more, God bless you my dearest Emma!

--------

Write your name on the back of the bill, if you send any person for the money.

I have scrawled three lines to Davison, that he should not think I neglected him in his confinement. I have received the inclosed from Allen. Can we assist the poor foolish man with a character?

As all our communication with Spain is at an end, I can now only expect to hear from my own dear Emma by the very slow mode of Admiralty vessels, and it is now more than two months since the 'John Bull' sailed.

I much fear, something has been taken, for they never would, I am sure, have kept me so long in the dark. However, by management, and a portion of good luck,, I got the account from Madrid in a much shorter space of time than I could have hoped for; and I have set the whole Mediterranean to work, and think the fleet cannot fail of being successful: and, if I had had the spare troops at Malta at my disposal, Minorca would at this moment have had English colours flying.

This letter, my dearest beloved Emma, goes — although in Mr Marsden's letter — such a roundabout way, that I cannot say all that my heart wishes. Imagine everything which is kind and affectionate, and you will come near the mark.

Where is my successor? I am not a little surprised at his not arriving! A Spanish war, I thought, would have hastened him. Ministers could not have thought that I wanted to fly the service, my whole life has proved the contrary: and, if they refuse me now: I shall most certainly leave this country in March or April; for few months' rest I must have, very soon. If I am in my grave, what are the mines of Peru to me!

But, to say the truth, I have no idea of killing myself. I may, with care, live yet to do good service to the State. My cough is very bad: and my side, where I was struck on the 14th of February, is very much swelled; at times, a lump as large as my fist, brought on, occasionally, by violent coughing, but I hope and believe, my lungs are yet safe.

Sir William Bolton is just arrived from Malta. I am preparing to send him a cruise, where he will have the best chance I can give him of making ten thousand pounds. He is a very attentive, good, young man.

I have not heard from Naples this age. I have, in fact, no small craft to send for news.

If I am soon to go home, I shall be with you before this letter.

May God bless you!

Thompson desires to be most kindly remembered to his dear wife and children. He is most sincerely attached to them, and wishes to save what he can, for their benefit.

As our means of communication are cut off, I have only to beg that you will not believe the idle rumours of battle, etc., etc., etc.

May Heaven bless you! prays, fervently, my dear Emma, ever your most faithful and affectionate,

*Nelson & Bronte*

I do assure you, my Dearest Emma, that nothing can be more miserable, or unhappy than your poor Nelson.

From the 19th of February, we have been beating from Malta to off Parma; where I am now anchored, the sea and wind being so contrary and bad. But I cannot help myself, and no one in the fleet can feel what I do; and, to mend my fate, yesterday Captain Layman arrived — to my great surprise — not in his brig, but in a Spanish cartel; he having been wrecked off Cadiz, and lost all the dispatches and letters.

You will conceive my disappointment! It is now from November 2nd that I have had a line from England.

Captain Layman says — he is sure the letters are sunk, never to rise again; but as they were not thrown overboard until the vessel struck the rock, I have much fear that they may have fallen into the hands of the Dons.

My reports from off Toulon, state the French fleet are still in port: but, I shall ever be uneasy at not having fallen in with them.

I know, my dear Emma, that it is vain to repine; but my feelings are alive to meeting those fellows, after near two years' hard service. What a time! I could not have thought it possible that I could have been so long absent; unwell and uncomfortable, in many respects.

However, when I calculate upon the French fleets, not coming to sea for this summer, I shall certainly go for dear England, and a thousand times dearer Merton. May heaven bless you, my own Emma!

I cannot think where Sir William Bolton is got to; he ought to have joined me, before this time.

I send you a trifle, for a birthday's gift — I would to God I could give you more: but, I have it not!

I get no prize-money worth naming; but, if I have the good fortune to meet the French fleet, I hope they will make me amends for all my anxiety; which has been, and is indescribable.

How is my little Horatia? I hope you have her under your guardian wing, at Merton. May God bless her!

Captain Layman is now upon his trial. I hope he will come clear, with honour. I fear it was too great a confidence in his own judgement that got him into the scrape; but it was impossible that any person living could have exerted himself more, when in a most trying and difficult situation.

Poor Captain Layman has been censured by the Court: but I have my own opinion. I sincerely pity him; and have wrote to Lord Melville, and Sir Evan Nepean, to try what can be done. All together, I am much unhinged.

To-morrow, if the wind lasts, I shall be off Toulon. Sir William Bolton is safe, I heard of him this morning. I hear, that a ship is coming out for him; but, as this is only rumour, I cannot keep him from this opportunity of being made post; and I dare say, he will cause, by his delay, such a tumble, that Louis's son, who I appointed to the 'Childers', will lose his promotion; and, then Sir Billy will be wished at the devil! But I have done with this subject; the whole history has hurt me. Hardy has talked enough to him, to rouse his lethargic disposition. I have been much hurt at the loss of poor Mr Girdlestone! He was a good man, but there will be an end of us all.

What has Charles Connor been about? His is a curious letter! If he does not drink, he will do very well. Captain Hilliar has been very good to him. Colonel Suckling, I find, has sent his son to the Mediterranean; taking him from the 'Narcissus' where I had been at so much pains to place him. I know not where to find a frigate to place him.

He never will be so well and properly situated again. I am more plagued with other people's business, or rather, nonsense, than with my own concerns.

With some difficulty, I have got Suckling placed in the 'Ambuscade', with Captain Durban, who came on board at the moment I was writing. The history of Suckling will never be done — I have this moment got from him your letter, and one from his father. I shall say nothing to him; I don't blame the child, but those who took him out of the most desirable situation in the Navy. He never will get into such another advantageous ship; but his father is a fool; and, so my dear Emma, that ends.

The box which you sent me in May 1804, is just arrived in the 'Diligent' store-ship.

I have sent the arms to Palermo, to Gibb's. The clothes are very acceptable; I will give you a kiss, for sending them. God bless you! Amen.

I am not surprised that we should both think the same about the kitchen; and, if I can afford it, I should like it to be done; but, by the fatal example of poor Mr Hamilton, and many others, we must take care not to get into debt; for then we can neither keep any of our relations, and must be for ever in misery! But, of this, we will talk more, when we walk upon the poop at Merton.

Do you ever see Admiral and Mrs Lutwidge? You will not forget me when you do.

To Mrs Cadogan, say everything that is kind; and to all our other friends; and, be assured, I am for ever and ever, yours and only yours,

Nelson & Bronte

"Victory" at Sea, May 16th, 1805

My Dearest Lady Hamilton,

As it is my desire to take my adopted daughter, Horatia Nelson Thompson, from under the care of Mrs Gibson, and to place her under your guardianship, in order that she may be properly educated and brought up, I have, therefore, most earnestly to entreat that you will undertake this charge; and as it is my intention to allow Mrs Gibson, as a free-will offering from myself, (she having no claim upon me, having been regularly paid for her care of the child) the sum of twenty pounds a year, for the term of her natural life; and I mean it should commence when the child is delivered to you. But should Mrs Gibson endeavour, upon any pretence, to keep my adopted daughter any longer in her care, then I do not hold myself bound to give her one farthing; and I shall, most probably, take other measures.

I shall write to Mr Haslewood, upon your telling him that you have received the child, to settle the annuity upon Mrs Gibson; and if you think Miss Conner disposed to be the governess of Horatia, I will make her any allowance for her trouble which you may think proper.

I, again and again, my dearest friend, request your care of my adopted daughter, whom I pray God to bless. I am ever, for ever, my dear Lady Hamilton, your most faithful and affectionate,

Nelson & Bronte

I sent, my own Dearest Emma, a letter to you, last night, in a Torbay boat, and gave the man a guinea to put it in the post-office.

We have had a nasty blowing night, and it looks very dirty.

I am now signalizing the ships at Plymouth to join me ; but I rather doubt their ability to get to sea. However, I have got clear of Portland, and have Cawsand Bay and Torbay under the lee.

I intreat, my dear Emma, that you will cheer up; and we will look forward to many, many, happy years, and be surrounded by our children's children. God almighty can, when he pleases, remove the impediment.

My heart and sole is with you and Horatia.

I got his line ready in case a boat should get alongside.

For ever, ever, I am yours most devotedly,

Nelson & Bronte

Mr Rose said, he would write to Mr Bolton, if I was sailed; but I have forgot to give him the direction: but I will send it today. I think, I shall succeed very soon, if not at this moment.

My Dearest Emma,

It is a relief to me, to take up the pen, and write you a line; for I have had, about four o'clock this morning, one of my dreadful spasms, which has almost enervated me.

It is very odd! I was hardly ever better than yesterday. Freemantle stayed with me till eight o'clock, and I slept uncommonly well ; but was awoke by this disorder. My opinion of its effect, some one day, has never altered. However, it is entirely gone off, and I am only quite weak. The good people of England will not believe, that rest of body and mind is necessary for me! But, perhaps, this spasm may not come again those six months. I had been writing seven hours yesterday; perhaps that had some hand in bringing it upon me.

I joined the fleet late on the evening of the 28th September, but could not communicate with them until the next morning.

I believe, my arrival was most welcome, not only to the commander of the fleet, but also to every individual in it; and, when I came to explain to them the Nelson touch, it was like an electric shock. Some shed tears, all approved — "It was new, it was singular, it was simple!" and, from Admirals downwards, it was repeated — "It must succeed, if ever they will allow us to get at them! You are, my Lord, surrounded by friends whom you inspire with confidence." Some may be Judas's; but the majority are certainly much pleased with my commanding them

*"Victory", October 19th, 1805*
*Noon, Cadiz, E.S.E., 16 Leagues*

*My Dearest Beloved Emma and the dear friend of my bosom,*

*The signal has been made that the enemy's combined fleet are coming out of the port.*

*We have very little wind, so that I have no hopes of seeing them before tomorrow. May the God of Battles crown my endeavours with success!*

*At all events I shall take care that my name shall ever be most dear to you and Horatia, both of whom I love as much as my own life, and as my last writing before the battle will be to you, so I hope in God that I shall live to finish my letter after the battle.*

*May Heaven help you, prays your Nelson & Bronte*

*October 20th in the morning we were close to the mouth of the Straights, but the wind had not come far enough to the westward to allow the combined fleets to weather the shoals of Trafalgar, but they were counted as far as forty sail of ships of war which I suppose to be 34 of the line, and six frigates.*

*A group of them was seen off the lighthouse of Cadiz this morning, but it blows so very fresh, I think (.....) weather, that I rather believe they will go into the harbour before night.*

*May God Almighty give us success over these fellows and enable us to get a Peace!*

This letter was found open in Lord Nelson's desk after the Battle of Trafalgar. When brought to Lady Hamilton she wrote on the last page:

O miserable, wretched Emma!
O glorious and happy Nelson!

# Epilogue

In 1814, there suddenly appeared in bookshops a publication entitled *'The Letters of Lord Nelson to Lady Hamilton; with a Supplement of Interesting letters by Distinguished Characters'* It was in two volumes and it was published anonymously. It is known that the books were printed by Macdonald and Son, Smithfield, for 'Thomas Lovewell & Co., Staines House, Barbican.' To this day, no one is certain who it was that published the letters. The ironically named 'Thomas Lovewell & Co' is not traceable.

The collection of letters eventually came into the possession of Mr Alfred Morrison, who included them in a further book published in 1893 entitled *'The Hamilton and Nelson Papers'.* After this the letters were split up.

In the year before they were published Lady Hamilton was in prison for debt. With no men left in her life to provide for her, her efforts to maintain a lifestyle to which she had become accustomed had finally caught up with her. And since they were her letters, then she was accused of selling them in order to raise money to get out of prison. The fact that, by the time they were published, she was not only out of prison but had fled to Calais, in France, seemed to bear out the accusation.

From Calais, in September 1814, she wrote to Sir William Scott, an old friend of her late husband, complaining that the pension that Sir William Hamilton had bequeathed her had not been paid, and neither had the pension left to her by Nelson from his Bronte estate in Sicily. At the bottom of this letter, Lady Hamilton added:

*'PS. I again before God declare I knew not of the publication of those stolen letters and I have taken the sacrament on it. Horatia sends her love'*

In other words, she was stating that whilst she was in prison, the letters were stolen from her. This might well be true, but it is known that Emma could also tell a good lie. The PS to her letter to Sir William Scott confirmed that she had with her in Calais, her daughter Horatia, whose father was Nelson. Although elaborate precautions and deceptions were employed to cover up the birth of their 'love child' in late January 1801, the letters confirm the reality. Horatia was fostered out from birth and, during the remaining years that Sir William Hamilton was alive, whilst they were all living together at Merton, she could only be brought to the house when Sir William was away. This was for the sake of *bienseance,* since the social code of the time was that 'affairs' were tolerated, so long as they were not flaunted. But, strangely, Emma Hamilton always insisted to Horatia that she was not, in fact, her true mother. She even made out that her true mother was none other than Maria Carolina, the Queen of Naples!

The letters also indicate that Emma was expecting a second child in March 1804. All the indications are that the child died at birth. What became of Emma's first daughter, 'little Emma' is not known. There is no record that Emma Hamilton kept in touch with her.

Emma Hamilton died on the 15 January 1815, just four months before her fiftieth birthday, and was buried at Calais.

Horatia went to live with Nelson's brother William, (the ambitious clergyman referred to as the 'Doctor' in the letters) who had inherited an Earldom and a pension of £5000 a year on behalf of his deceased brother. She then went to live with Nelson's sister, Mrs Matcham. She married a clergyman, the Rev. Philip Ward, in 1822 and they had seven children. Horatia died in 1881 and never acknowledged that she was the daughter of Emma, Lady Hamilton, only that she was the daughter of Lord Nelson.

# Chronology (1793-1815)

1793    War declared between Britain and France.
Nelson sails for Mediterranean in the *Agamemnon*.
First meeting with the Hamilton's at Naples. Stays for five days.

1794    Land actions on Corsica. Nelsons loses sight of right eye.

1795    Nelson takes French ship *Ca Ira*. Sir John Jervis appointed Commander-in-Chief of Mediterranean fleet.

1796    Jervis appoints Nelson commodore. Nelson hoists flag on *Captain*. Spain joins with France against Britain. Orders given to British fleet to withdraw from Mediterranean.

1797    February 11th, upon leaving Mediterranean, Nelson sails through Spanish fleet undetected. Re-joins with English fleet off Cape St. Vincent, Portugal. Jervis decides to engage his 15 ships against Spanish fleet of 27. Nelson disobeys orders but becomes hero of the battle. Made Knight of the Bath and promoted to rear admiral. Sent to capture treasure ship at Tenerife. Attempt fails. Nelson loses right arm. Returns to England to recuperate.

1798    January, advises Admiralty ready for active service. Hoists flag on *Vanguardd*, sent back into Mediterranean to find and destroy French fleet. August 1st, finds French fleet anchored in Aboukir Bay, mouth of the Nile. Destroys all but two of French fleet. Returns to Naples, stays with Hamilton's. Made Baron Nelson of the Nile.
King Ferdinand raises army - marches into Rome on November 26th.
French counter attack re-takes Rome in December.

Nelson assists King and Queen of Naples and Hamilton's to flee to Sicily.

1799    January, the French take Naples. Lord Keith appointed C-in-C, Mediterranean. Nelson and Lady Hamilton become lovers. Nelson disobeys orders to sail to Minorca. Created Duke of Bronte by King Ferdinand. Naples recaptured in June. Rebels executed. August, Bonaparte escapes from Egypt.

1800    Nelson captures French ship *Le Genereux* that escaped from the Nile. Sir William Hamilton retires. Nelson returns to England through Europe with the Hamilton's. Arrive at Great Yarmouth 6th November.

1801    January 1st, appointed vice-admiral and second in command of the Channel fleet. Splits with wife. January 13th, hoists flag on the *St Josef.* Lady Hamilton gives birth to daughter, Horatia,. January 30th.
Battle of Copenhagen. Created Viscount Nelson. Buys Merton Place in Surrey. October 22nd given leave and joins Hamilton's at Merton.

1802    Peace treaty with France. Nelson's father dies. July and August, Hamilton's and Nelson tour Midlands and South Wales.

1803    April 6th, Sir William Hamilton dies. War with France declared. Nelson hoists flag on *Victory* and appointed C-in-C of Mediterranean fleet. Joins fleet at Toulon in July. Bonaparte prepares to invade England.

1804    Nelson scans Mediterranean for French fleet. Spain joins with France against Britain.

1805    April 4th, news reaches Nelson that French fleet has left Mediterranean.

Nelson pursues French fleet to West Indies and back.

Arrives back in England 18th August after two years at sea.
Rejoins fleet September 28th at Cadiz. Killed at Battle of Trafalgar October 21st. News of Trafalgar victory reaches England November 6th.

1806 January 8th, state funeral procession. January 9th, state funeral service in St. Paul's Cathedral. Nelson's brother created Earl.

1809 Emma, Lady Hamilton sells Merton Place. Mrs Cadogan, Emma's mother, dies.

1813 Lady Hamilton in debtor's prison. Robert Southey's *Life of Nelson* published.

1814 Lady Hamilton flees to France with Horatia. Anonymous publication of Nelson's letters to Lady Hamilton.

1815 Lady Hamilton dies at Calais. Horatia returns to England and lives with Nelson's family.

# Bibliography

Fraser, Flora, *Beloved Emma* (1986)

Gamlin, Hilda, *Nelson's Friendships* (1899)

Harris, David, (Ed) *The Nelson Almanac* (1998)

Kennedy, Ludovic, *Nelson's Band of Brothers* (1951)

Morriss, Roger, Nelson – *The Life and Letters of a Hero* (1997)

Oman, Carola, *Nelson* (1947)

Pocock, Tom, *Horatio Nelson* (1987)

Russell, Jack, *Nelson and the Hamiltons* (1969)

Sichel, Walter, *Emma, Lady Hamilton* (1905)

Southey, Robert, *The Life of Nelson* (1813)

White, Colin, (Ed) *The Nelson Companion* (1995)